Eyewitness
DINOSAUR

In association with
THE NATURAL HISTORY MUSEUM

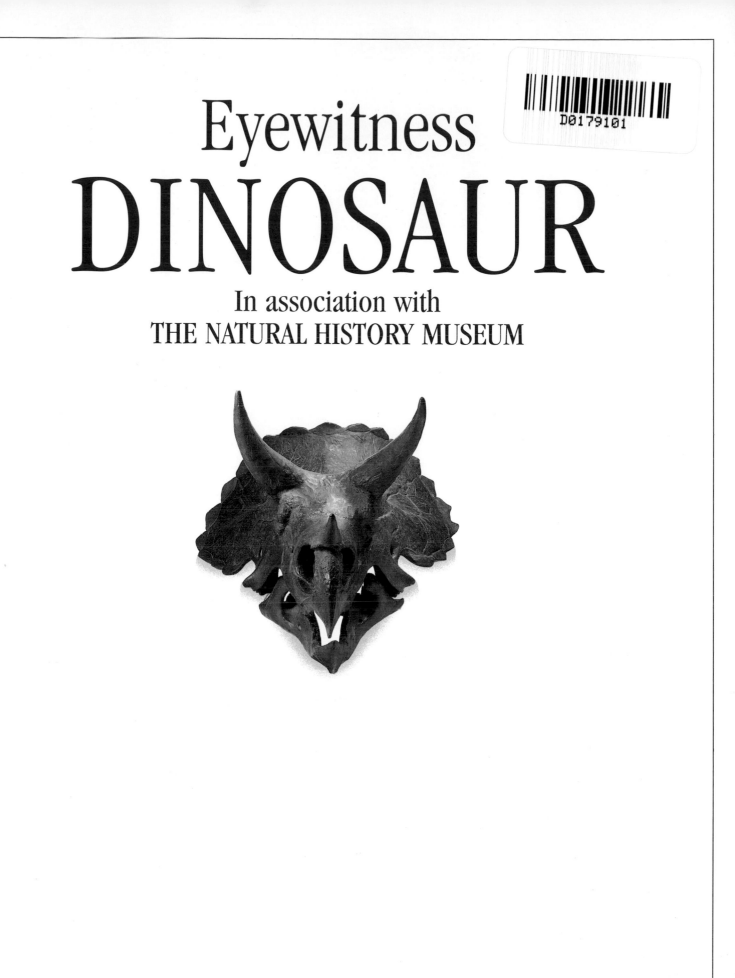

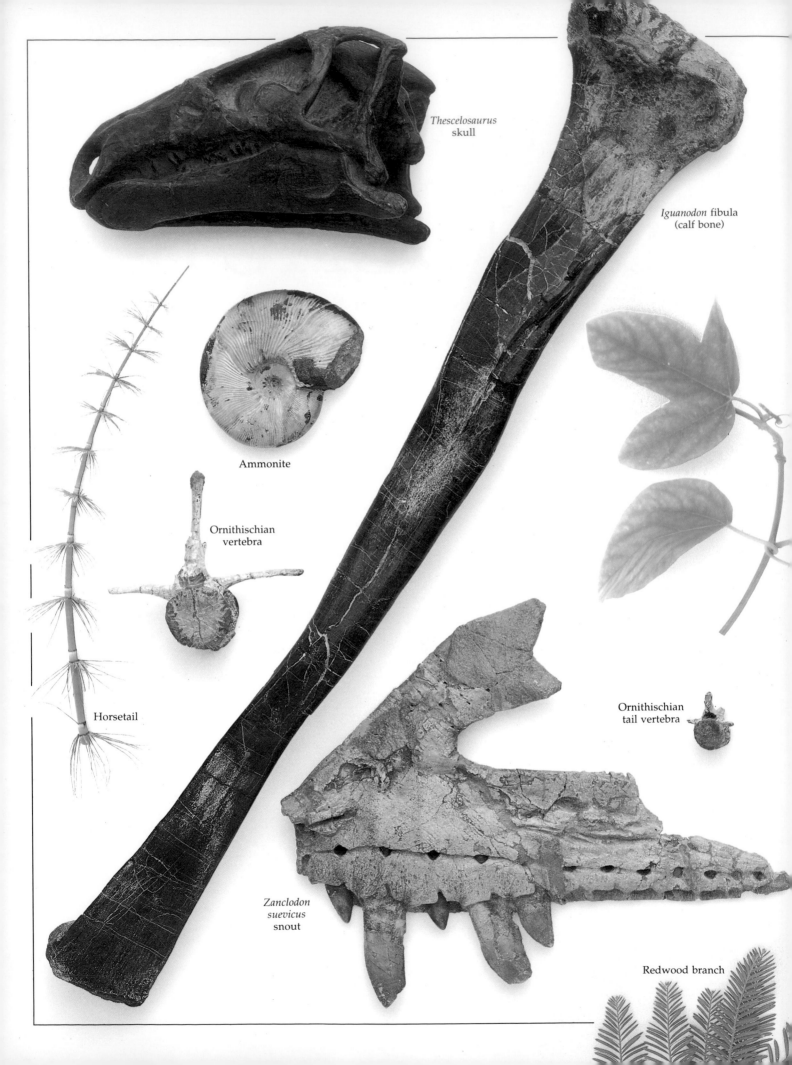

Thescelosaurus skull

Iguanodon fibula (calf bone)

Ammonite

Ornithischian vertebra

Horsetail

Ornithischian tail vertebra

Zanclodon suevicus snout

Redwood branch

Stegosaur tooth

Chirostenotes claw

Dogwood leaves

Eyewitness
DINOSAUR

In association with
THE NATURAL HISTORY MUSEUM

Written by
DR DAVID NORMAN
AND
DR ANGELA MILNER

Passionflower leaves

Albertosaurus claw

Gizzard Stones

Cross-section of *Iguanodon* tail vertebra

Hadrosaur teeth

Megalosaurus tooth

DK

Hypsilophoon vertebrae

Ginkgo leaves

Coelurosaur neck vertebra

Hadrosaur toe bone

Dryosaurus femur (thigh bone)

DK

LONDON, NEW YORK, MELBOURNE, MUNICH, and DELHI

Project editor Susan McKeever
Art editor Lester Cheeseman
Senior editor Sophie Mitchell
Senior art editor Miranda Kennedy
Managing editor Sue Unstead
Managing art editor Roger Priddy
Special photography Colin Keates

PAPERBACK EDITION
Managing editors Linda Esposito, Andrew Macintyre
Managing art editors Jane Thomas, Martin Wilson
Publishing manager Sunita Gahir
Category publisher Andrea Pinnington
Art director Simon Webb
Editors Clare Hibbert, Sue Nicholson
Art editors Andrew Nash, Joanna Pocock
Consultants Dougal Dixon, Michael Benton
Production Jenny Jacoby, Angela Graef
Picture research Celia Dearing
DTP designers Siu Chan, Andy Hilliard, Ronaldo Julien

This Eyewitness ® Guide has been conceived by
Dorling Kindersley Limited and Editions Gallimard

First published in Great Britain in 1989
Revised edition published in 2007 by
Dorling Kindersley Limited,
80 Strand, London WC2R 0RL

This edition produced in 2008 for The Book People,
Hall Wood Avenue, Haydock, St. Helen's, WA11 9UL

A CIP catalogue record for this book is
available from the British Library.

ISBN 978-1-40533-101-2

Colour reproduction by Colourscan, Singapore
Printed in China by Toppan Co., (Shenzhen) Ltd.

Ornithomimus toe

Monkey puzzle branch

Tyrannosaurus rex tooth

Morosaurus chevron bone

Discover more at
www.dk.com

Contents

Heterodontosaurus skull

What were the dinosaurs?

BACK IN THE MISTS OF TIME, there lived an extraordinary group of animals. Called dinosaurs, they survived for more than 150 million years, and then disappeared off the face of the Earth in the most mysterious extinction ever. Many of them were gigantic, but some were tiny, the size of a chicken. Some were peaceful and ate only plants; others were fierce sharp-toothed flesh eaters. Dinosaurs were reptiles, just like the living iguana lizard on this page. They had scaly skin and laid eggs. But unlike the lizard, which has short, sprawling legs, dinosaurs had long legs tucked under their bodies, which meant that they could move much more efficiently. Many other reptiles shared the dinosaur world, swimming in the sea and flying in the air, but dinosaurs lived only on land. We know about them today because their bones and teeth have been preserved in rock as fossils.

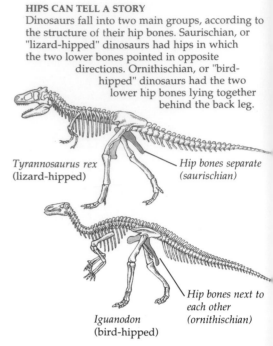

HIPS CAN TELL A STORY
Dinosaurs fall into two main groups, according to the structure of their hip bones. Saurischian, or "lizard-hipped" dinosaurs had hips in which the two lower bones pointed in opposite directions. Ornithischian, or "bird-hipped" dinosaurs had the two lower hip bones lying together behind the back leg.

Tyrannosaurus rex
(lizard-hipped)

Hip bones separate
(saurischian)

Hip bones next to
each other
(ornithischian)

Iguanodon
(bird-hipped)

Iguana lizard

DINOSAURS COULDN'T FLY!
Flying reptiles, like the pterosaurs shown here feeding on a *Triceratops* carcass, shared the dinosaur world, but were not dinosaurs. No dinosaur could fly.

Sharp claws

Characteristic
scaly skin

Dinosaurs
may have
been this
colour

Nostril

LIVING DINOSAUR?
The tuatara is a rare, endangered species of reptile
found only on islands off the coast of New Zealand.
Extinct relatives of the tuatara lived during the
dinosaur age. The spines on its back are reminiscent
of some dinosaurs' back spines.

HOW DINOSAURS EVOLVED
The nearest living reptile relatives of dinosaurs are
crocodiles. Millions of years ago, an ancient
crocodile-like ancestor, or thecodontian ("socket-
toothed reptile") developed the habit of running on
land. Over millions of years thecodontians changed
the way they moved their legs, became smaller,
faster moving, and eventually evolved into the
earliest dinosaurs.

IN THE WATER
Proterosuchus was
an early thecodontian
that spent most of its time in the water.

ON FOUR LEGS
Thecodontians like
Euparkeria left the
water to live on land,
walking on all-fours.

"BIRD CROCODILE"
Ornithosuchus
was a later,
predatory
thecodontian that walked on two
legs - a cousin of the first
dinosaurs.

**UPRIGHT AND
DANGEROUS**
Staurikosaurus was
one of the earliest dinosaurs. A
flesh eater, its fully upright gait
made it a fast mover, giving it an
advantage over the thecodontians
before it.

Neck frill

WHAT'S LEFT. . .
One of the earliest dinosaurs to be
discovered was named after an iguana
(pp. 8-9). Green and scaly, this iguana
looks prehistoric, and indeed has
features in common with some dinosaurs,
like the texture of the skin, and the
sharp claws.

Short sprawling legs

Early discoveries

Iguanodon tooth from lower jaw

DINOSAUR MAN
This cartoon shows Sir Richard Owen, the man who invented the name Dinosaur. He is sitting astride a giant ground sloth (a fossil mammal that was found in South America).

ALTHOUGH DINOSAUR remains have been around for millions of years, people knew nothing about these extraordinary creatures until the 19th century. One of the first people to discover dinosaur bones was an English doctor called Gideon Mantell, who collected rocks and fossils as a hobby. In 1820 Dr Mantell, with his wife Mary Ann, found some large teeth embedded in stone. Mantell had never seen teeth quite like them before, and when he found some bones nearby, he began to do some serious research into the find. After a lot of work, Dr Mantell concluded that the teeth and bones had belonged to some kind of giant reptile, which he named *Iguanodon*, meaning "Iguana tooth" (pp. 6-7). Two other giant reptiles were discovered in Britain soon afterwards, named *Megalosaurus* and *Hylaeosaurus*. But it was not until 1841 that these creatures were given a group name. An eminent scientist of the time, Sir Richard Owen, declared that they should be called "Dinosaurs", meaning "terrible lizards". Thus began an exciting time of discovery in the scientific world. The great dinosaur hunt was on.

Tooth from upper jaw

Worn edge

THE FIRST TEETH
Still embedded in the gritty stone in which they were found by the Mantells, are the original *Iguanodon* teeth. The top edges of the dinosaur's teeth were worn down by chewing plants (pp. 26-27).

Horn on nose was actually a thumb spike

Long whiplash tail like an iguana lizard

A ROUGH SKETCH
Dr Mantell had discovered a collection of bones and teeth. But what on earth had the owner of the bones looked like when it was alive? Mantell pictured it as a gigantic lizard, a bit like an iguana. He drew a picture of it perched on a branch, with its thumb spike (of which he had found only one) placed on its nose!

Gideon Mantell's original drawing of *Iguanodon*

Part of an *Iguanodon* backbone

Backbones fused together

THE DISCOVERER
Although he was a medical doctor by profession, Gideon Mantell was an enthusiastic collector of rocks and fossils. Soon his home looked like a museum as his collection grew.

MORE BONES
More bones from *Iguanodon* found by Gideon Mantell include this portion of the backbone which fitted between the hips of the animal.

DINNER IN A DINOSAUR
As the interest in dinosaurs grew, a great display of giant models was mounted in the gardens of London's Crystal Palace. Before the *Iguanodon* model was finished, the sculptor held a dinner party inside it for 20 people.

Iguanodon tibia (shin bone)

MONSTERS IN THE PARK
These two concrete models of *Iguanodon* were made by the sculptor Benjamin Waterhouse Hawkins in the last century. Although inaccurate - *Iguanodon* looked nothing like this (p. 39) - they can be seen to this day in the park at Crystal Palace, London.

Dinosaur landscape

Dınosaurs lived on the Earth for over 150 million years, and it is not surprising that their world changed substantially during this time. Continents, at first just one great landmass, gradually drifted apart until they resembled the modern arrangement that we are familiar with. This meant that the climate changed as well, and both these factors influenced the types of plants that grew. These changes happened slowly over millions of years and animals adapted accordingly. At the beginning of the dinosaur age, low shrubby fern-like plants dominated the landscape. Then came a time when huge coniferous forests and groves of cycads flourished. Later on, the biggest change of all happened when the first flowering plants began to appear. Many plants and flowers that the dinosaurs may have eaten can still be seen growing today.

FIR FEAST
Herbivorous dinosaurs had ample vegetation to satisfy their appetites. Duckbilled dinosaurs, such as *Parasaurolophus*, above, could cope with tough plants because their jaws and teeth were so powerful. Even fir needles posed no problem.

ANCIENT PUZZLE
Living monkey puzzle trees are relatives of ones which flourished long before dinosaurs ever trod the Earth.

CYCAD FROND
Cycads were abundant during most of the dinosaur reign, and are still to be seen today, although they are quite rare.

A DINOSAUR HOME
This scene shows the type of landscape that would have been familiar to dinosaurs of about 130 million years ago. Horsetails, ferns, and cycads abound.

Conifer:
Pseudotsuga menziesii

Passion flower:
Passiflora sp.

Holly:
Ilex aquifolium

THE FLOWERING
The first flowering plant appeared
during the last period of the dinosaurs'
reign. Flowering plants can reproduce more
quickly than other types, and they rapidly
came to dominate plant communities
worldwide. Flowers changed the diets of
dinosaurs dramatically.

Cycad:
Cycas revoluta

Ginkgo:
Ginkgo biloba

A MAGNOLIA
It is surprising to
think of dinosaurs
eating flowers, but
when magnolias
appeared about
100 million years
ago they were no doubt
munched upon by many
plant-eating dinosaurs.

Cherry Laurel:
Prunus laurocerasus
"Otto Luykeres"

Magnolia:
Magnolia loebneri

Fern:
Marattia werneri

Fern:
Blechnum sp.

Horsetail:
*Equisetum
giganteum*

Dogwood:
Cornus alba

Little and large

A LOT OF PEOPLE think of dinosaurs as being massive creatures, big enough to reach the treetops, but there were also tiny dinosaurs, ones that would not even reach your knee. The biggest creatures ever to walk the Earth were the sauropod group of dinosaurs, which were all plant eaters. For a long time, *Brachiosaurus* was the biggest sauropod that we knew much about. Weighing about 70 tons, it was 22 m (70 ft) long, and stood at 12 m (39 ft) high - about as tall as a four-storey building. But now bones have been found belonging to even larger dinosaurs. *Paralititan*, found in Africa, was about the same weight as *Brachiosaurus* but could have been up to 30 m (100 ft) long. *Argentinosaurus*, found in South America, was around 40 m (130 ft) long and probably weighed as much as 20 large elephants. By contrast with these quite peaceful giants, the tiny dinosaurs like *Compsognathus* (far right) were mostly agile, crafty meat eaters, some no heavier than a cat.

AS TALL AS A HOUSE
This French engraving shows a popular image of dinosaurs as giants: an alarming visitor to a Paris street investigates a balcony on the fifth floor of a tall building.

THE OWNER OF THE BONE
This *Brachiosaurus* is the type of dinosaur that owned the massive leg bone (far right). The huge, pillar-like forelimbs were longer than the hindlimbs - probably to help it to reach up to the treetops for food.

FANTASTIC FEMUR
The femur (upper leg bone) shown right belonged to a *Brachiosaurus*. If you stood next to a *Brachiosaurus* leg, you would hardly reach past its knee bone! The gentleman (left) is examining an *Apatosaurus* femur, which measures 2.1 m (6 ft 2 in) long. *Apatosaurus* was another type of sauropod dinosaur.

Part of a large *Brachiosaurus* femur, ending in knee joint

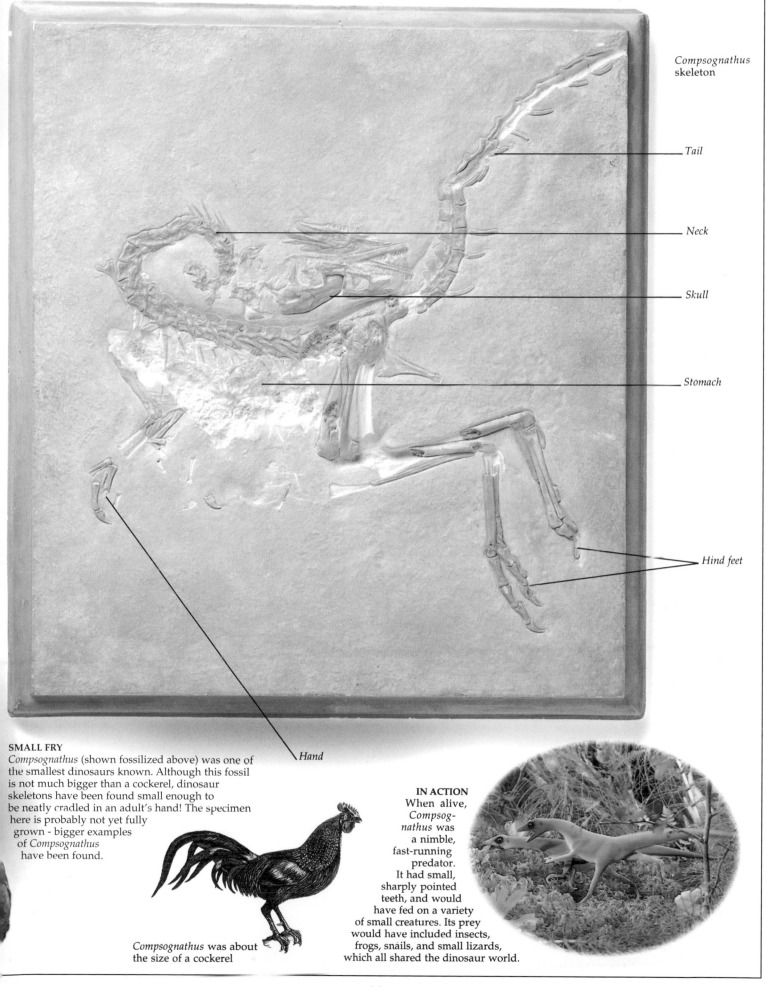

Compsognathus skeleton

Tail

Neck

Skull

Stomach

Hind feet

Hand

SMALL FRY
Compsognathus (shown fossilized above) was one of the smallest dinosaurs known. Although this fossil is not much bigger than a cockerel, dinosaur skeletons have been found small enough to be neatly cradled in an adult's hand! The specimen here is probably not yet fully grown - bigger examples of *Compsognathus* have been found.

Compsognathus was about the size of a cockerel

IN ACTION
When alive, *Compsognathus* was a nimble, fast-running predator. It had small, sharply pointed teeth, and would have fed on a variety of small creatures. Its prey would have included insects, frogs, snails, and small lizards, which all shared the dinosaur world.

The long-necked beast

THE MASSIVE CREATURE that can be seen spread across the next eight pages was one of the biggest dinosaurs ever to walk the Earth. It was called *Diplodocus*, and like *Brachiosaurus*, below, it belonged to a group of dinosaurs called sauropods (p. 12). *Diplodocus* looked extraordinary with its long neck and tail, and a head that was tiny in proportion to the rest of its body. This type of body suited its lifestyle perfectly. It could reach up to feed at the tops of the very tall trees, like conifers, that grew at the time. Its small head allowed it to browse amongst the vegetation, where few other dinosaurs could reach. This type of feeding needed a special type of neck - one that was strong, light, and flexible, in order to be raised and lowered easily. Having stripped one area bare of food, it would have ambled off with its companions in search of new feeding grounds. If *Diplodocus* was threatened by a meat eater, its only defence would have been its bulk, and its long, whip-like tail (pp. 20-21).

Small skull compared to size of body

NECK SUPPORT
This head and neck belong to *Brachiosaurus*. Like *Diplodocus*, it must have had powerful neck muscles that could raise its head. It would also have needed a strong heart to pump blood at high pressure so that it could reach the brain.

SHORT AND FLEXIBLE
Unlike *Diplodocus*, a predator such as *Tyrannosaurus rex* (left) needed a neck that was short, powerful, and flexible. It had to be short to support the large vicious head. Flexibility in the neck meant that *Tyrannosaurus rex* could twist its head around to wrench flesh from its prey.

A HARD NECK
Triceratops' neck (left) needed to be short and extremely strong in order to support the weight of its head. As well as using the force of its head to wrench off tough vegetation, it also fought and charged enemies with its three formidable horns (pp. 30-31).

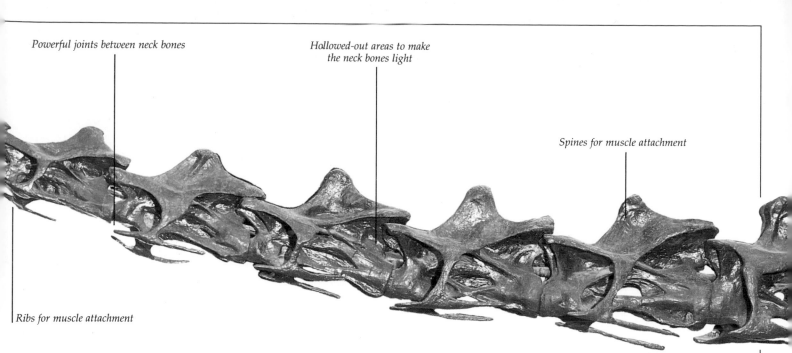

Powerful joints between neck bones

*Hollowed-out areas to make
the neck bones light*

Spines for muscle attachment

Ribs for muscle attachment

JURASSIC BROWSERS

Due to its enormous size, *Brachiosaurus* must have spent most of its time
eating. Travelling as part of a herd, the dinosaur would have fed in
riverside forests and open woodland containing conifers, cycads, and ferns.
Its fossil remains have been found in Africa, Europe, and America. By
swinging its long neck, *Brachiosaurus* could reach the leaves of tall trees.
Lowering it, the dinosaur could nibble at low-growing ferns.

The beast continues. . .

CRANING THE NECK
The design of a *Diplodocus* neck is
rather like that of a man-made
crane. The jib, which juts out from
the main tower and from which the
hooks used for lifting things are
suspended, is like the dinosaur's
neck. The heavy base of the crane
which keeps it from toppling over
is like *Diplodocus'* sturdy body. The
jib of a crane has to be light and
strong, so the engineer builds it
with a light metal framework.
Diplodocus had lightweight, but
very strong bones in its neck, which
it could raise and lower just like the
jib of a crane.

Neck bone

The backbone story

The body of *Diplodocus* was designed to bear and move enormous weight, and the backbone, between shoulders and hips, was the powerhouse of the whole animal. The backbones had to be strong enough to support the enormous weight of the neck, tail, and belly. They were also hollowed out, however, for lightness. Narrow spines, pointing upwards from the top of the backbone, acted as anchor points for powerful back muscles. Long ribs pointing downward curved around the belly, helping to hold the backbone in position against the great weight of the belly, and protecting the internal organs of the animal.

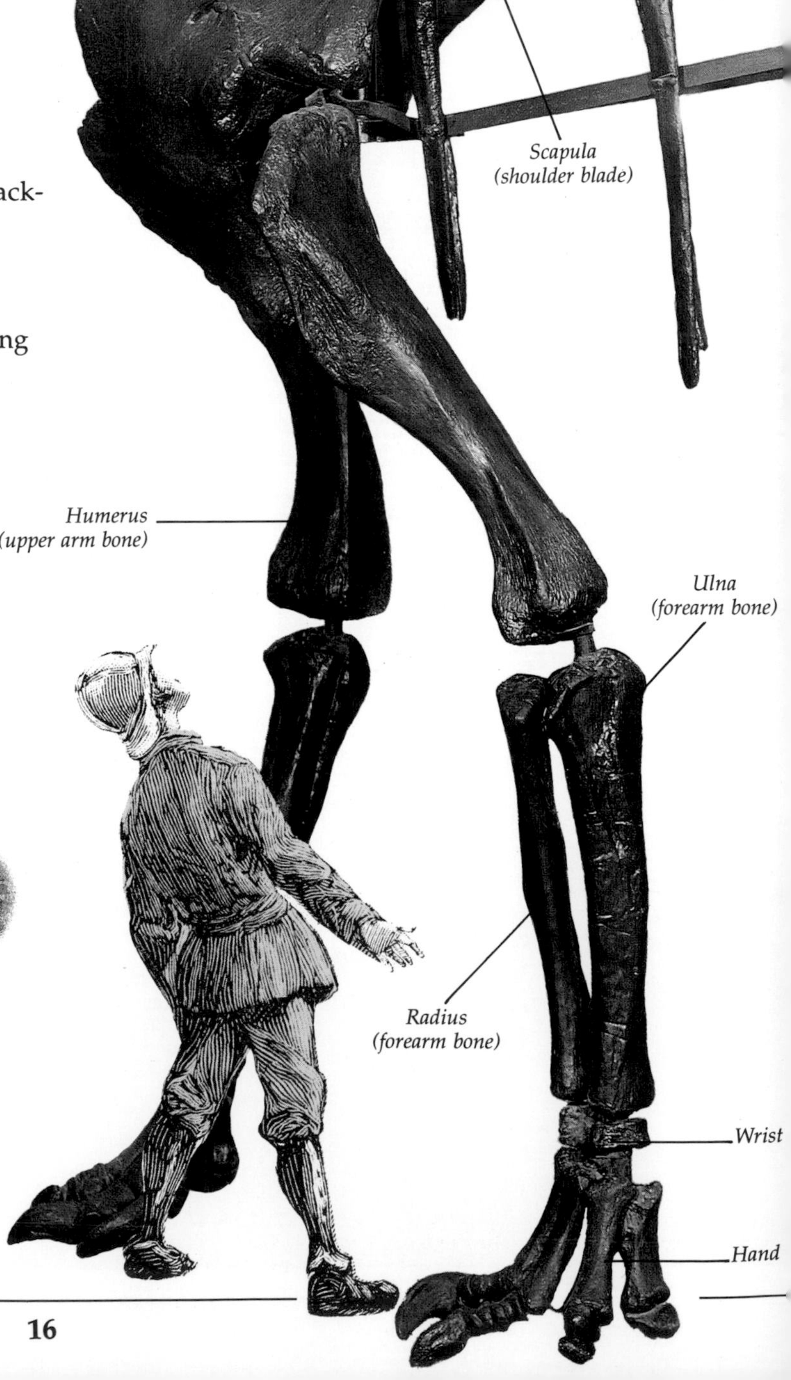

Scapula
(shoulder blade)

Humerus
(upper arm bone)

Ulna
(forearm bone)

Radius
(forearm bone)

Wrist

Hand

Temple of Jupiter, Athens

LEGS LIKE PILLARS
The strong legs of *Diplodocus* supported its body just as the pillars of this Greek temple support the heavy stone roof. The limb bones were heavy and dense, capable of supporting the enormous weight of the dinosaur.

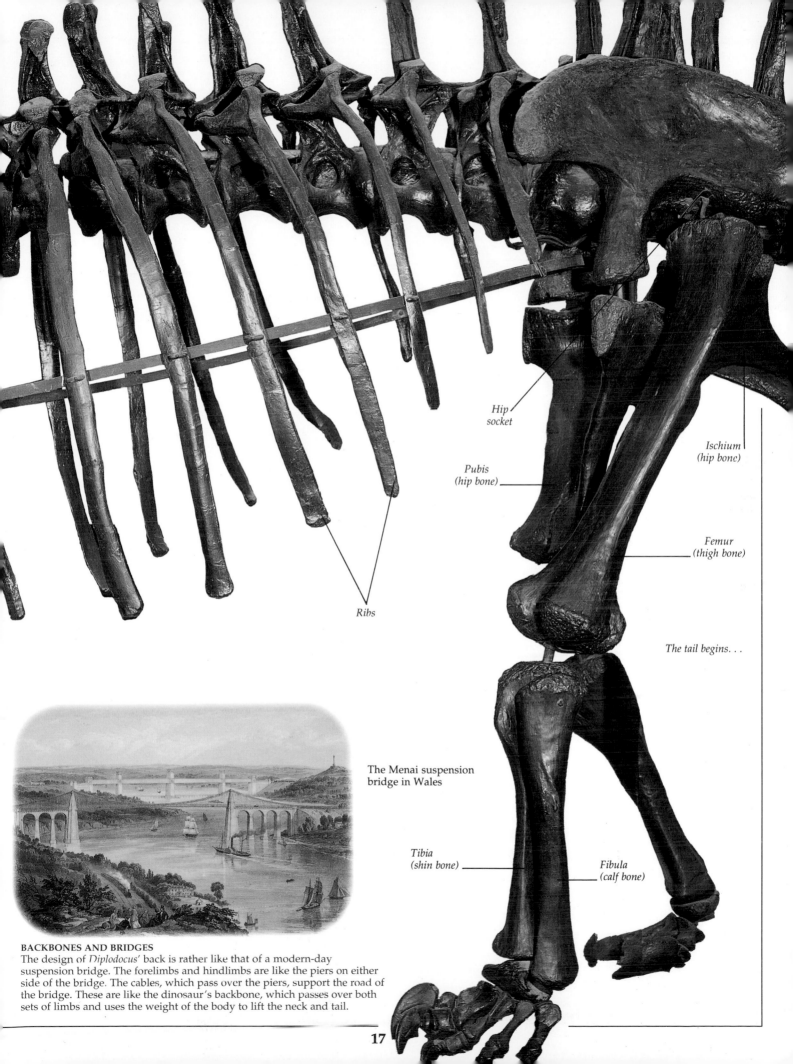

Hip
socket

Ischium
(hip bone)

Pubis
(hip bone)

Femur
(thigh bone)

The tail begins. . .

Ribs

The Menai suspension
bridge in Wales

Tibia
(shin bone)

Fibula
(calf bone)

BACKBONES AND BRIDGES
The design of *Diplodocus'* back is rather like that of a modern-day
suspension bridge. The forelimbs and hindlimbs are like the piers on either
side of the bridge. The cables, which pass over the piers, support the road of
the bridge. These are like the dinosaur's backbone, which passes over both
sets of limbs and uses the weight of the body to lift the neck and tail.

Kangaroos sometimes rest or groom themselves while sitting on their hind legs, using the tail as a balancing aid. They also balance on their tails while fighting. Leaning only on the tail, they can kick out with their feet, as in this picture. They do not usually wear boxing gloves, however!

Kangaroo and boxer engaged in combat

Ischium (hip bone)

Elongated chevron

All about tails

Tails can have a surprising number of uses. The most important one for living reptiles, as well as dinosaurs, is that it provides an anchor point for the attachment of large leg-moving muscles, running from the sides of the tail bones to the top of the hind leg. Sauropod dinosaurs such as *Diplodocus* may have used their tails for balancing. By rearing up and balancing on hind legs and tail, they would have extended their reach into the treetops, perhaps gaining access to better-quality food. Fast moving two-legged dinosaurs used their tails to balance while running.

Chevron bones become more flattened towards the middle of the tail

Diplodocus rearing up on its hind legs to feed

BALANCING ACT
Until recently, scientists believed that sauropods could only walk on all-fours. But experts who have studied the size and strength of the legs, and the tail structure, agree that sauropods often reared up on their hind legs to feed.

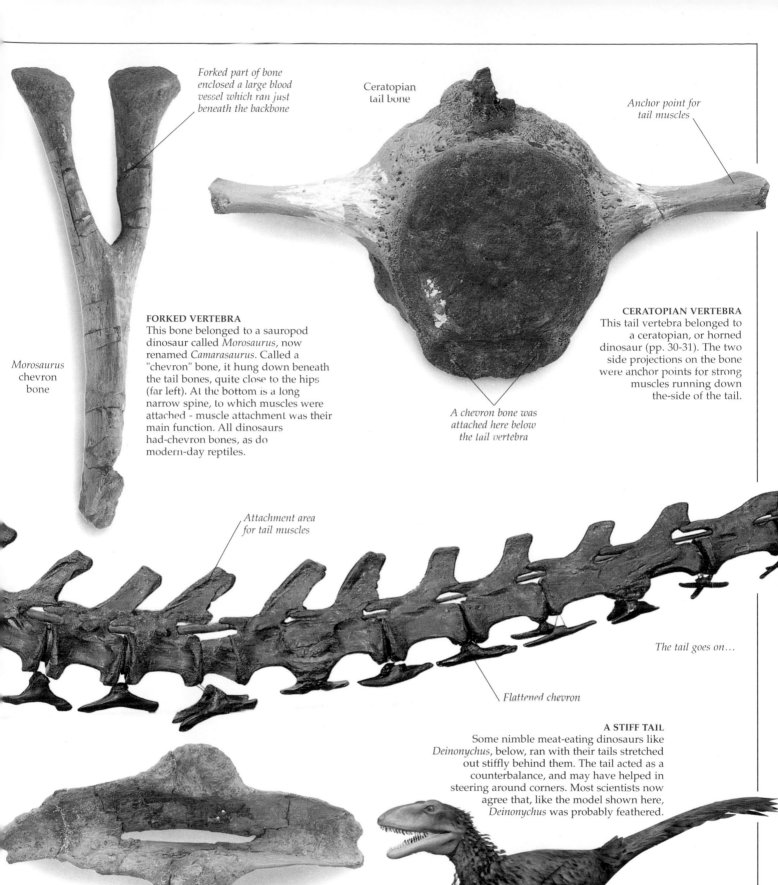

Forked part of bone enclosed a large blood vessel which ran just beneath the backbone

Ceratopian tail bone

Anchor point for tail muscles

Morosaurus chevron bone

FORKED VERTEBRA
This bone belonged to a sauropod dinosaur called *Morosaurus*, now renamed *Camarasaurus*. Called a "chevron" bone, it hung down beneath the tail bones, quite close to the hips (far left). At the bottom is a long narrow spine, to which muscles were attached - muscle attachment was their main function. All dinosaurs had-chevron bones, as do modern-day reptiles.

CERATOPIAN VERTEBRA
This tail vertebra belonged to a ceratopian, or horned dinosaur (pp. 30-31). The two side projections on the bone were anchor points for strong muscles running down the-side of the tail.

A chevron bone was attached here below the tail vertebra

Attachment area for tail muscles

The tail goes on…

Flattened chevron

A STIFF TAIL
Some nimble meat-eating dinosaurs like *Deinonychus*, below, ran with their tails stretched out stiffly behind them. The tail acted as a counterbalance, and may have helped in steering around corners. Most scientists now agree that, like the model shown here, *Deinonychus* was probably feathered.

Diplodocus chevron bone

Deinonychus

DIPLODOCUS CHEVRON
Towards the middle of *Diplodocus*' tail, the chevron bones became more flattened and boat shaped, like this one, photographed from above. These types of chevron bones may have acted as skids to protect the underside of the tail as it dragged along the ground.

The tale of defence

TAILS WERE A VERY USEFUL MEANS of defence for many plant-eating dinosaurs, and what they lacked in teeth and claws was compensated for by their ingenious tails. Some dinosaurs, like the sauropods, had long, thin tails which they used as whiplashes. Apart from their daunting size, this was their main form of defence. Armoured dinosaurs, or ankylosaurs, had bony clubs on their tails, as well as being protected from head to toe with body armour. Stegosaurs, or plated dinosaurs (pp. 34-35), sported formidable sharp tail spikes which they used to lash out at attackers. Some modern-day reptiles use their tails in self-defence: crocodiles will lash out at an enemy with their heavy, scale-covered tails, and many lizards have long whiplash-type tails. No living reptiles, however, have defensive tails with attachments as spectacular as the terrifying spikes and clubs used by some dinosaurs to defend themselves.

WALKING THORN BUSH
This armoured dinosaur, *Gastonia*, was the length of a large car. Unlike fellow ankylosaur *Euoplocephalus* (below right), *Gastonia* did not have a heavy tail club. However, big spines could have made its tail a formidable weapon. The rest of *Gastonia*'s body was also studded with sharp, defensive spines.

Tail bones

Joint between tail bones

Tail bones become narrower towards the end

Scelidosaurus

Bony studs

Long muscular tail

USEFUL TAIL
Scelidosaurus was a plant eater that relied mostly on its armoured skin to protect it from predators. But its long tail may have given it an extra advantage. It could have used it to balance while it reared up on hind legs in order to run away from a pursuing meat eater.

THORNY DEVIL
Some living reptiles, like the Moloch lizard, above, are so well armoured from head to toe that they don't need a special defensive tail. Few predators would attempt an attack on this spiky lizard. It lives in dry or desert areas of Australia.

Some lethal tails

All the dinosaurs that used their tails in defence were four-footed and herbivorous (p. 26). Those dinosaurs that walked on two legs, like the duckbills (p. 28) needed their tails to balance, so they had no clubs or spikes. They had to rely on speed or camouflage for defence. The whiplash used by some sauropods, like *Diplodocus*, would have annoyed large meat eaters, and probably caused quite a stinging pain. The fearsome-looking clubs and spikes belonging to the ankylosaurs and stegosaurs were often used as a silent threat - rather like saying "don't come any closer!"

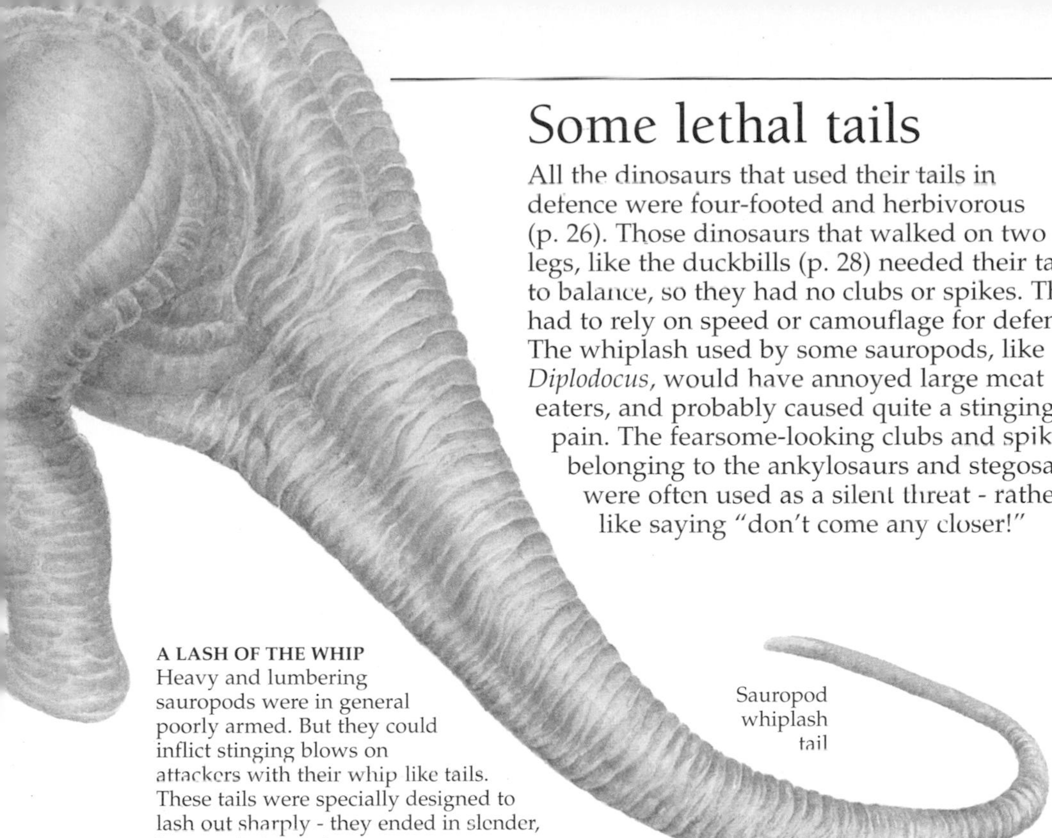

Stegosaurus tail spike

A LASH OF THE WHIP
Heavy and lumbering sauropods were in general poorly armed. But they could inflict stinging blows on attackers with their whip like tails. These tails were specially designed to lash out sharply - they ended in slender, bony rods (see below).

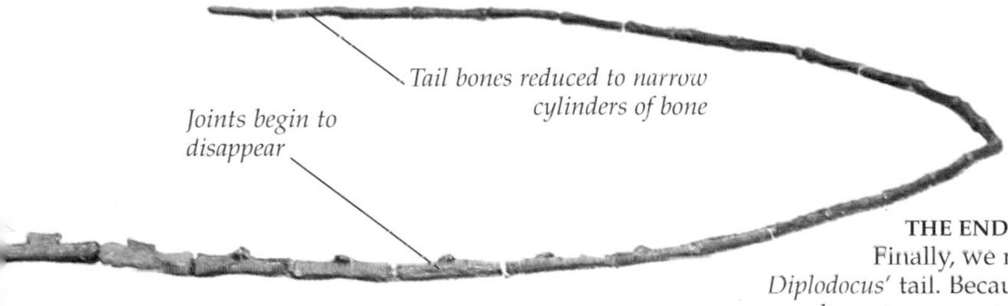

Sauropod whiplash tail

Rough area for attachment of horny covering

Tail bones reduced to narrow cylinders of bone

Joints begin to disappear

THE END OF THE TAIL
Finally, we reach the end of *Diplodocus'* tail. Because they did not have to support any muscle, the bones at the tip have become narrow cylinders. This also makes the tail into an effective whiplash.

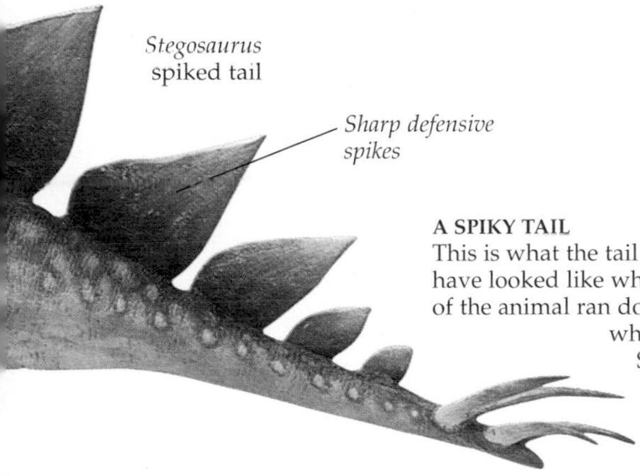

Stegosaurus spiked tail

Sharp defensive spikes

A SPIKY TAIL
This is what the tail spikes of *Stegosaurus* would have looked like when attached. The bony plates of the animal ran down the tail to meet the spikes, which were confined to the tip. So when the tail was swished to the side, the tip was the part that moved fastest, causing the most damage.

Euoplocephalus clubbed tail

CLUBBED TAIL
This armoured dinosaur's tail ended in a huge, heavy, bony club. This was made out of several chunks of bone, all welded together into a single lump. The club sometimes measured as much as 1 m (3 ft) across. The dinosaur, called *Euoplocephalus*, would have needed very powerful and flexible tail muscles in order to swing such a tail around and to drive the club into an enemy.

SPIKE STORY
Shown here at half life-size, this *Stegosaurus* tail spike (pp. 34-35) would have been covered by a tough layer of horn in life, and sharply pointed at the end. Swung against the soft underbelly of a meat eater, it would have inflicted a terrible, crippling wound.

Dinosaur diets

MANY OF US IMAGINE DINOSAURS as being fearsome meat-eating creatures. But some were peaceful plant eaters that simply browsed amongst the treetops, tearing off leaves. Other dinosaurs were able to eat a mixed diet of meat and plants, as humans do. Those that were not vegetarian did not confine themselves to dinosaur meat. They would have eaten anything that moved, including insects and birds. Fossilized dinosaur remains can tell us a lot about what the animal ate when it was alive. The most important clues are to be found in the shape and arrangement of the jaws and teeth. Even the overall shape of a dinosaur's body tells a story - meat eaters often had big heads and short, powerful necks in order to wrench lumps of meat off a kill. The long necks of many plant eaters were useful for reaching up to the treetops to feed.

BY THE RIVER
This early 20th-century illustration depicts a scene from 190 million years ago, with meat-eating dinosaurs, swimming reptiles, and flying pterosaurs all sharing the same landscape. But although these creatures did all exist at that time, it is unlikely that prehistoric reptiles would have thronged together in this way.

VEGETARIAN SKULL
This skull belonged to a huge plant eater, or herbivore, called *Diplodocus*. All of the thin, pencil-like teeth are at the front of the mouth. *Diplodocus* would have used them like a rake to draw in fern leaves and other vegetation. Unable to chew, *Diplodocus* simply swallowed what it raked in.

Orbit (eye socket)

Pencil-like teeth

Weak lower jaw

Diplodocus skull

SERIOUS TEETH
The fearsome rows of curved, serrated teeth in the *Allosaurus* skull (below) are typical of carnivores (meat eaters). The "windows" in the massive skull helped to reduce its weight. *Allosaurus* may well have fed on the young of herbivores such as *Diplodocus* (opposite). An adult *Diplodocus* would have been too big to tackle, unless *Allosaurus* hunted in packs.

Large cavity in front of eye for jaw muscles

Orbit (eye socket)

Large serrated teeth

Allosaurus skull

Powerful lower jaw

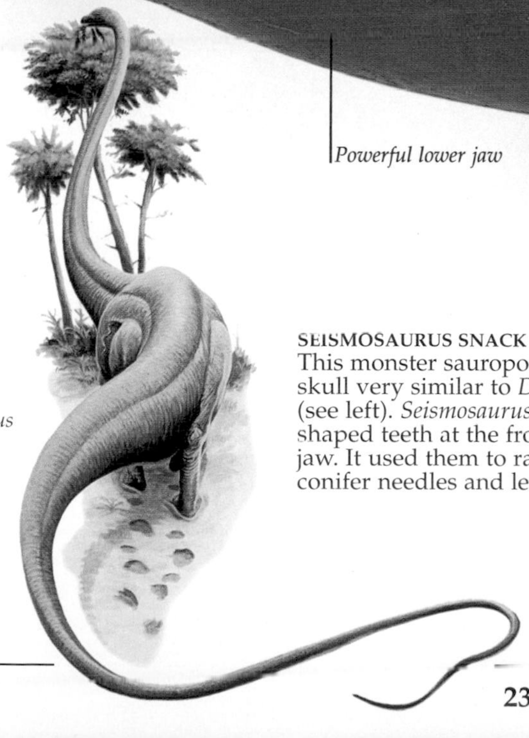

Seismosaurus

SEISMOSAURUS SNACK
This monster sauropod had a skull very similar to *Diplodocus'* (see left). *Seismosaurus* had peg-shaped teeth at the front of its jaw. It used them to rake in conifer needles and leaves.

Massospondylus skull (below)

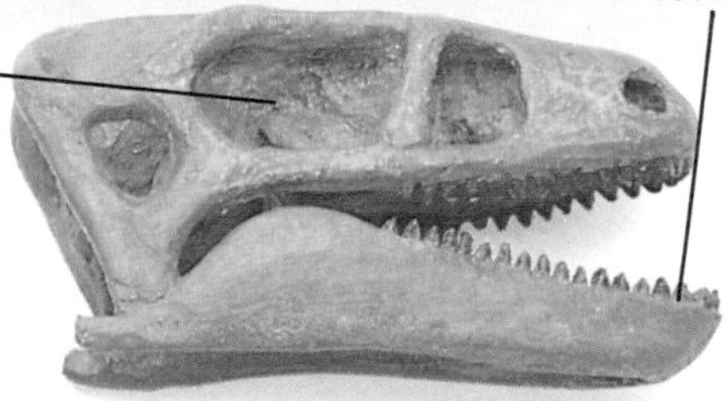

Small coarse teeth

Orbit (eye socket)

DUAL DIET DINOSAUR
The skull above belonged to *Massospondylus*. Its teeth, being neither serrated and stabbing, nor rake-like or grinding, were "multi-purpose". Small and coarse-edged, they could chew either meat or plants. Animals who can eat like this are called omnivores.

Meat eaters

ALL THE MEAT-EATING DINOSAURS belonged to a group called Theropoda, which literally means "beast footed". Some of the meat-eating dinosaurs were called carnosaurs or "flesh lizards" - large animals with big heads, powerful legs, and short arms. Like all theropods, they walked on two legs, probably not very fast because of the bulk they had to carry. They had big heads to accommodate long jaws which were lined with huge curved teeth, serrated like steak knives. Carnosaurs pursued and ate other dinosaurs, or else fed on corpses that they found. They would kill their prey with the help of their clawed feet and then tear off the flesh of the victim with their hands - well-equipped with sharp claws - and teeth. The other meat eaters were known as coelurosaurs, or "hollow-tailed lizards". By contrast with the carnosaurs, they were lightly built nimble creatures with long grasping arms and hands, and long, narrow jaws. They could run very fast, in order to catch small mammals and insects. After a carnosaur had eaten its fill, a coelurosaur would often move in to eat the scraps that were left.

SMALL BUT VICIOUS
It is hard to believe that a dinosaur tooth (left) could be smaller than a human incisor, or cutting-tooth (right). This dinosaur tooth belonged to *Troodon*, or "wounding tooth".

The king

Tyrannosaurus rex is probably the best known (and most feared) of the carnosaurs. A formidable 12 m (39 ft) long, it had a massive skull with powerful jaws that held serrated teeth up to 18 cm (7 in) long. It probably used its tiny arms to push itself upright after it had been lying down.

Backward-curving teeth gave carnosaurs a better grip on a victim

Gorgosaurus lower jaw

NUTHETES TOOTH
Still embedded in rock, this tooth came from a small meat eater called *Nuthetes*.

SMALLER GNASHER
Not all tyrannosaur teeth were huge. This small one is curved, in order to hook into its victim.

LION'S SLICER
Meat-eating animals, like lions, have developed special slicing teeth. No dinosaur had a tooth like this.

NEW GNASHER
Meat-eating dinosaurs' teeth kept growing and were constantly replaced throughout life. This megalosaur tooth is a "new" one.

The large, curved tooth of *Megalosaurus*

Fine serrations like those on a steak knife

Cracks which occurred during fossilization

A LOSING BATTLE?
A Victorian etching shows *Iguanodon* (left) and *Megalosaurus* (right) fighting each other. Although *Iguanodon* has been given sharp teeth by the artist, it was in fact a plant eater, and would not have stood much chance against the might of *Megalosaurus*. The spike on its nose was really on its thumb in life, and was its only real weapon of defence (pp. 8-9).

THE BIGGEST...
This large *Megalosaurus* tooth is of a typical carnosaur shape, with its curved edge pointing backwards. The edges of the tooth are sharp, with saw-like serrations for cutting meat. The cracks on this specimen appeared during fossilization.

Ceratosaurus skull (below)

Sharp serrated front edge of tooth

Bony tooth socket

Inner side of jaw bone

LETHAL JAW BONE
This *Gorgosaurus* lower jaw (left) stretched the length of the animal's skull. Powerful jaw muscles, reaching up behind the eye, were attached to the area without teeth. These would have produced a powerful bite, snapping the jaw shut on impact with its prey. The skull above, which belonged to another carnosaur, shows the same basic design.

Plant eaters

TINY TEETH
This jaw came from *Echinodon*, one of the smallest plant-eating dinosaurs. The tiny teeth had spiky edges, like those of an iguana lizard, which eats a mixed diet of plants and meat.

MANY OF THE DINOSAURS were plant eaters, including the biggest of all, the sauropods (pp. 12-13). Eating a diet of plants causes animals many more problems than eating meat. Plants are made of tough materials like cellulose and woody lignin, and need to be broken down before digestion can take place in the animal's stomach. Plant-eating dinosaurs coped with their diet in a variety of ways: the sauropods did not chew at all, but simply swallowed raked-in vegetation. This passed directly to the stomach, and was ground up by deliberately swallowed "gizzard stones" (gastroliths), or fermented by bacteria, as in a cow's stomach. The hadrosaurs, or duckbilled dinosaurs, had special teeth which ground and chopped their food before they swallowed it. Ceratopians tackled tough plants with their extra-strong jaws and scissor-like teeth. All of the bird-hipped dinosaurs (p. 6) were plant eaters.

Plant-eating dinosaurs would have eaten conifers such as this yew leaf

Main jaw bone

Ceratopian beak

SCISSOR TOOTH
This tooth came from a ceratopian dinosaur, like *Triceratops* (below). After tearing off the vegetation with its beak (far left), it would then have sliced it up with its sharp teeth.

Notch for replacement tooth to slot in

Cycad plant

TOUGH AND STRINGY
Some experts believe that ceratopian dinosaurs evolved specially to eat new kinds of tough plants. They would have eaten the leaves of palm-like cycads (left), and maybe even tackled pine cones (above).

Pine cone

BUILT TO CHEW
Dinosaurs like this *Triceratops* (pp. 30-31) ate tough, fibrous plants (above). *Triceratops*, like many ceratopians, had extremely powerful jaws and sharp teeth to help it to cope with its diet.

CROPPING BEAK
A beak like this ceratopian one (p. 30) was ideal for cropping tough plants. The rough grooves and pits mark the place where the horny covering of keratin was attached. The lower, wider part of the bone (called the predentary) fitted tightly against the lower jaw.

THE GREATEST GRINDER

Duckbilled dinosaurs had the most spectacular array of teeth of any plant-eating dinosaur. Hundreds of sharp, diamond-shaped teeth lined both sides of upper and lower jaws. The grinding surface formed by a duckbill's battery of teeth acted like a chopping board, or a self-sharpening vegetable grater, which crushed the plants. New teeth constantly grew to replace the worn ones, as can be seen here, pushing up the top layer of teeth in this *Edmontosaurus* jaw (below).

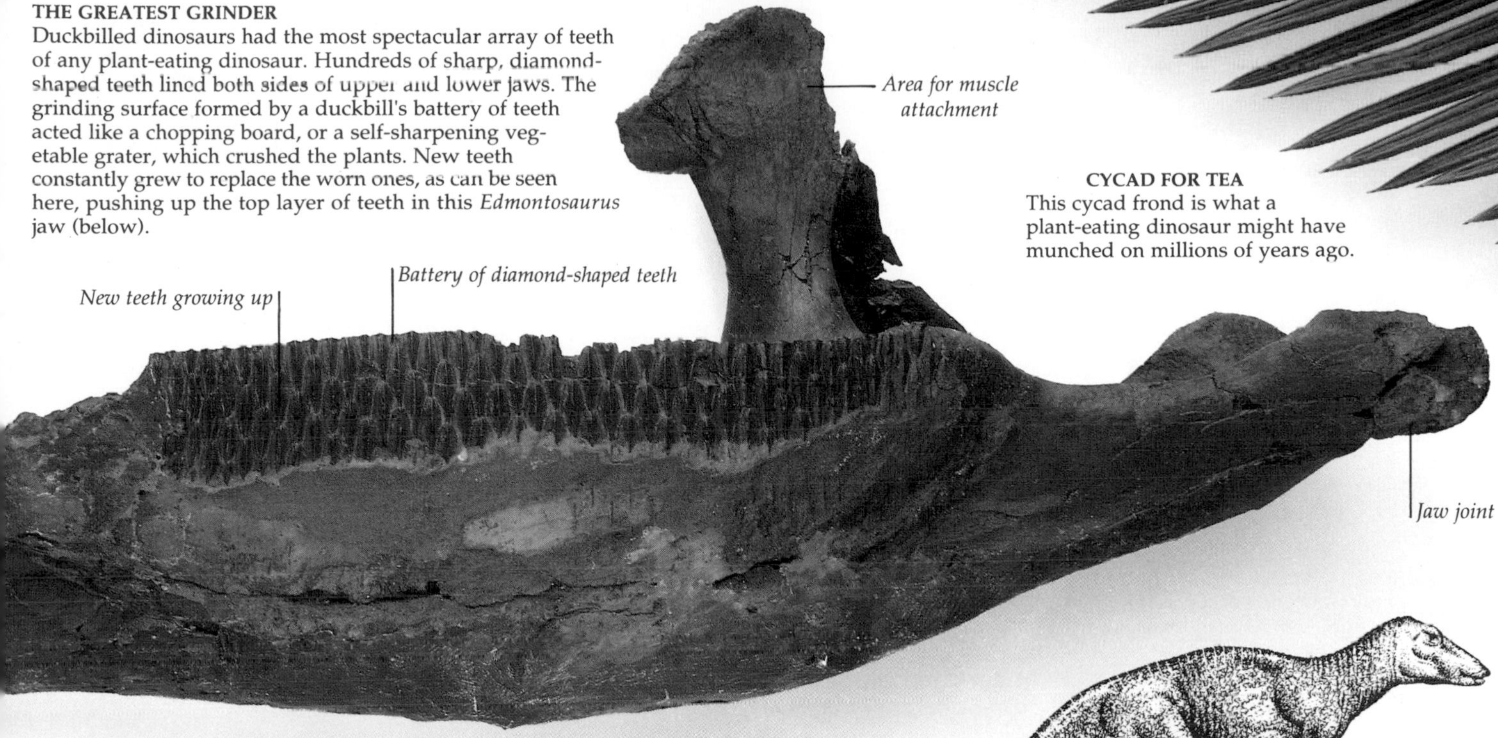

Area for muscle attachment

CYCAD FOR TEA

This cycad frond is what a plant-eating dinosaur might have munched on millions of years ago.

New teeth growing up

Battery of diamond-shaped teeth

Jaw joint

Edmontosaurus jaw

Sharp edge of tooth for nipping

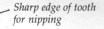

Area worn down by eating plants

Edmontosaurus

BELLOWING BEAST

An *Edmontosaurus*, which owned the jaw above, looked like this. It had about 1,000 strong teeth in its cheek region. It may have blown up the loose skin on its flat face to make a loud bellowing call. Duckbilled dinosaurs could also store extra food in their cheeks, like hamsters.

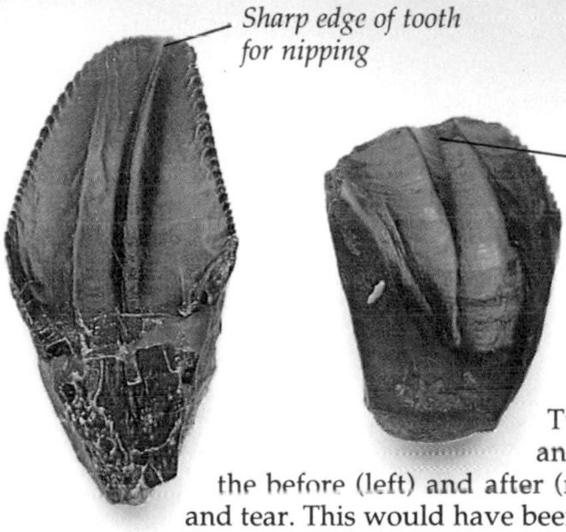

WEAR AND TEAR

Two lower teeth of an *Iguanodon* show the before (left) and after (right) stages of wear and tear. This would have been caused by the rough plant materials cellulose and lignin. Added to this was the inevitable grit and dust that the animal would have eaten along with the plant.

FOOD FOR THOUGHT

Some of the plants that the dinosaurs used to eat still grow today. These include cycads, horsetails, ferns, and pine trees (pp. 10-11).

Fern leaf

Ankylosaur tooth

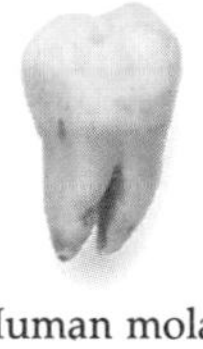

Human molar

Sauropod peg-like tooth

Pine needles

DENTAL SELECTION

Sauropods' teeth were either spoon-shaped, for nipping, or peg-like, for raking in leaves. The ankylosaurs, or armoured dinosaurs (p. 33), had small teeth which were only good for eating soft plants. No dinosaur had flat teeth like human molars, which we use to crush and grind our food.

Sauropod spoon-like tooth

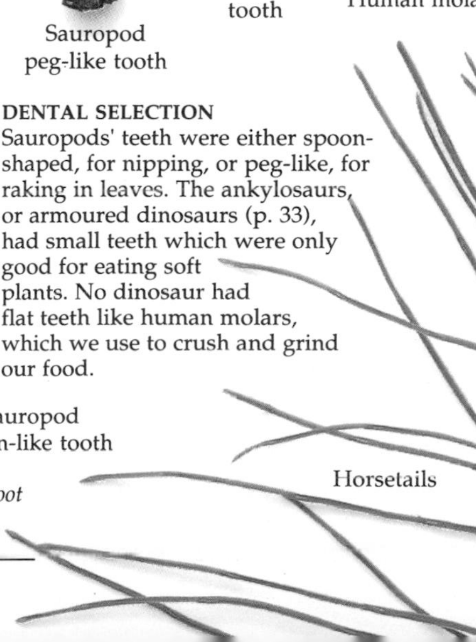

Root

Horsetails

27

Peculiar heads

The first two heads in this selection are duckbills: *Parasaurolophus*, with its distinctive long horn, and *Corythosaurus* with its "dinner-plate" shaped crest. The broad, thick head on the right belongs to *Pachycephalosaurus*, one of the "bone-headed" dinosaurs.

SOME DINOSAURS HAD most oddly shaped heads, sprouting weird and wonderful projections of bone including lumps, bumps, crests, spikes, and helmets. And just as bizarre shapes or brightly coloured patches on reptiles, birds, and even mammals today attract attention, so did the odd shapes of some dinosaurs' heads. They were eye-catching, and could have been used to attract a mate, scare off an enemy, or simply indicate how a dinosaur was feeling - happy or angry! They were often used in attack or defence - a bony head could act like a natural safety-helmet, or a formidable head-butting device. The most spectacular heads belonged to a group of dinosaurs called the hadrosaurs, or duckbills, so-called because of their broad, toothless beaks.

CREST FALLEN
Different hadrosaurs had different head shapes, but their bodies were all quite similar. Some had heads that were completely unadorned with odd-looking projections. This drawing from 1897 shows one of the most common "crestless" types, *Edmontosaurus*. It used its broad, duck-like beak to scoop up leaves.

Toothless beak

Teeth start here

Parasaurolophus skull

Long crest was hollow inside

Dome of solid bone

GIVING A HOOT
The long hollow crest on the skull of
Parasaurolophus has puzzled experts for
years. At first it was thought to be a "snorkel",
or a reserve air tank used when the animal was
feeding under water. Or perhaps it was an extension
of the nostrils, enhancing the creature's sense of smell.
Now we know that the hollow tube was probably a
"resonator", through which the dinosaur could bellow
or hoot in a distinctive way. Females of this species
had smaller, less spectacular crests.

Bony spike

THE HEADBANGER
The head of *Pachycephalosaurus*
(meaning "thick headed reptile")
was 80 cm (2 ft 7 in) long, and its dome
was made of solid bone. It used this
dome to head-butt enemies, just as
sheep and goats use their horns.

Pachycephalosaurus skull

REARING TO GO
Pachycephalosaurus may
well have reared up and
bellowed loudly, as in the
picture, before charging
an enemy.

Sharp, pointed beak

Psittacosaurus skull

DUCKBILL DINNER
Because hadrosaurs had toothless beaks,
they were often pictured wading in
swamps, and feeding on soft water
plants. But in reality they were
mainly land feeders, and could
tackle tough vegetation
from trees, grinding
it up with their
powerful jaws (p. 26).

Parasaurolophus
feeding

PARROT HEAD
This oddly shaped skull
belonged to a *Psittacosaurus*,
or "parrot lizard". Although it
did not have many teeth, its sharp,
deep beak could slice through tough
leaves and woody stems.

BIRD BEAK
Psittacosaurus had a sharp beak like a
parrot, but there the similarity ended!

Three-horned face

Triceratops, which means "three-horned face", belonged to a group of dinosaurs known as ceratopians, or horned dinosaurs. Each ceratopian had a large bony frill pointing backwards from the skull and masking the neck, horns on the nose or over the eyes, and a narrow, hooked beak. Most were four-legged and stocky, like the rhinoceroses of today, and all were plant eaters. Many fossils of ceratopians found in the same area suggest that they roamed in herds, confronting a threatening meat eater as a pack. As the ceratopians evolved, their headgear gradually became more pronounced. *Triceratops*, the "king" of the ceratopians, lived at the end of the reign of the dinosaurs, and had the most spectacular array of horns and frills of all the ceratopians: its head took up nearly one-third of its length. With head lowered and the horns pointing forward, all backed up by its enormous bulk, *Triceratops* must have provided a formidable defence to predators such as *Tyrannosaurus rex* (p. 24).

LIKE A RHINO
This model reconstruction of *Triceratops*, based on the study of complete skeletons of the animal, is probably very close to life. Here, the resemblance to modern rhinoceroses is very striking.

Brow horn

Nose horn

Nostril

Parrot-like beak

Wavy edge of frill

Triceratops skull - front view

SKULL STORY
By far its most prominent feature, *Triceratops*' heavy skull can tell us a lot about its way of life. Its jaw was built to tackle very tough and fibrous plant matter. It used its narrow hooked beak to snip off plants, which it then sliced up with its sharp, scissor-like teeth. Huge muscles which extended up into the frill powered the jaws. The frill probably acted as an anchor for the jaw muscles, and also protected the neck. *Triceratops* used its sharp horns mainly for defence against tyrannosaurs, but it also used them in one-to-one combat. The male *Triceratops* would lock horns with a member of its own kind and head-wrestle, much as deer, antelope, and sheep do today.

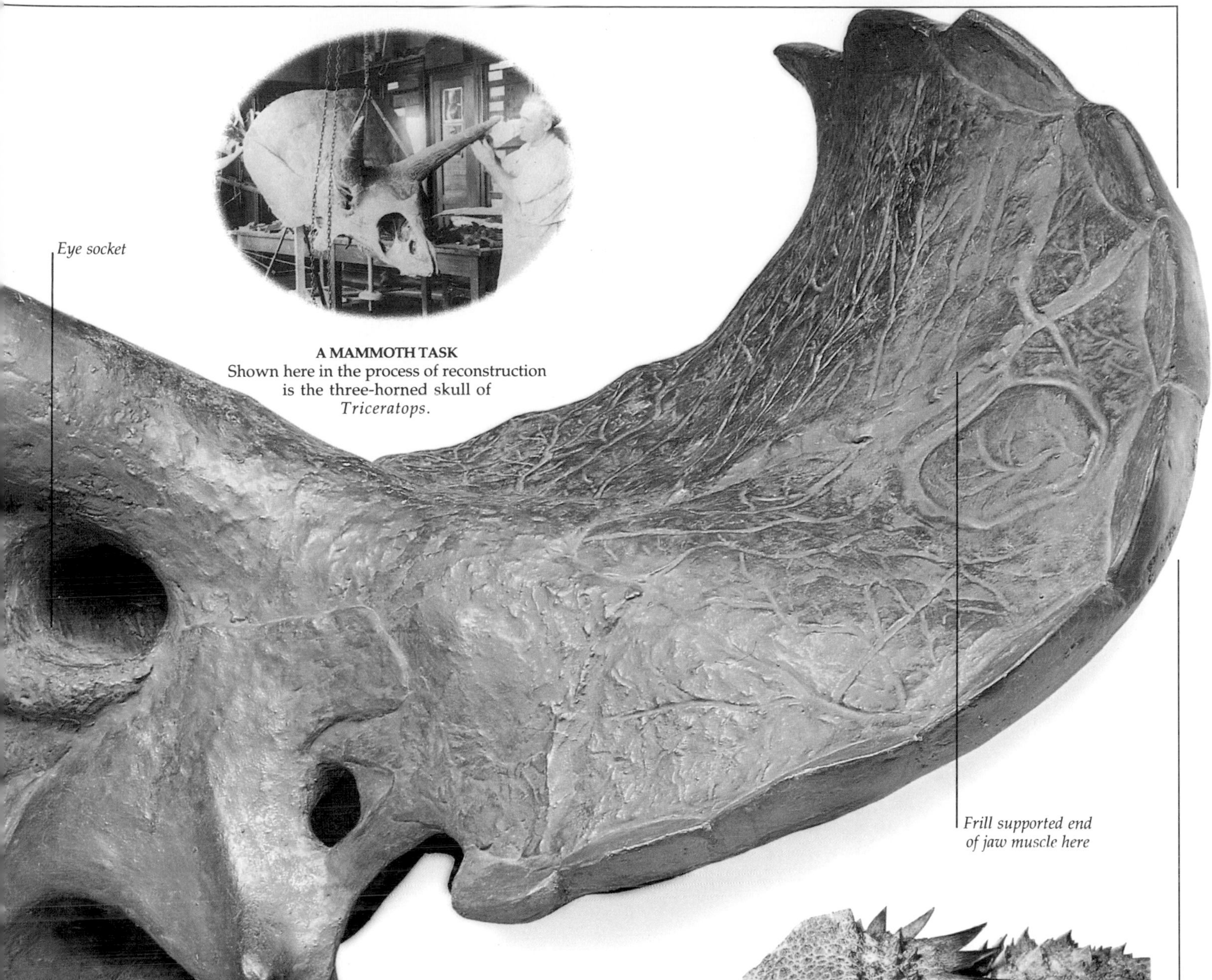

Eye socket

A MAMMOTH TASK
Shown here in the process of reconstruction
is the three-horned skull of
Triceratops.

*Frill supported end
of jaw muscle here*

Triceratops
skull - side view

*Jaw muscle was
attached here*

Regal
horned lizard

PRESENT-DAY FRILL
Some living lizards, like this
regal horned lizard, have horns
and frills too. Lizards use their
frills to intimidate enemies,
expanding them to make
themselves look larger than
they really are.

SPIKY STYRACOSAURUS
Roughly half the length of
Triceratops but no less impressive
was *Styracosaurus*. It, too, had
an enlarged nose horn, and its
frill had extra-long spikes, as
well as several smaller ones.
Styracosaurus would have looked
very imposing if it lowered its head in display.

A tough skin

WHAT WAS dinosaur skin like? Fossilized skin impressions can tell us that it was scaly, like reptile skin, and in some cases armour-plated for extra protection. Dinosaur skin was perfectly suited to life on land. Just like reptile skin, it was waterproof, tough, and horny. Waterproof skin prevents an animal from drying out quickly in air, sun, or wind - animals like frogs have to stay in moist conditions because their skin is thin and not waterproof. Tough, scaly skin protects an animal while it moves about on land, dragging the body over, or between, rough stones, or falling over. Dinosaur skin impressions, like the ones shown here, are usually small, because after death, animal skin rots away too quickly to be fossilized. However, in a few rare cases, an almost entire body impression has been preserved. The dinosaurs that left these impressions probably died in a dry area so that their skin became dried out, before being buried by wind-blown sand. The sand then turned into sand-stone over the years, and was so tightly packed against the skin that when the skin disappeared, its exact shape and pattern remained in the stone. No one knows for sure what colour dinosaur skin was, or whether it had stripes or spots - dinosaurs are most often shown in "muddy" shades of green and brown.

COLOUR CO-ORDINATED
Dinosaurs may well have had brightly coloured skin like this agamid lizard. Skin colour can be useful as camouflage, or as a warning signal. This lizard probably uses his bright-green skin to mark out a territory, or to attract a mate.

ARMOUR-PLATED MAMMAL
Well protected by its bony armour, the armadillo that lives today is like the ankylosaurs, or armoured dinosaurs (right). They, too, stayed low to the ground while predators were threatening. Few attackers would have been able to get a grip on their tough bodies.

SOLITARY NODULE
Bony nodules like this one were mixed in with the overlapping plates on *Polacanthus* skin. These nodules "floated" in the skin beneath the scales, as in living reptiles.

Polacanthus skin impression

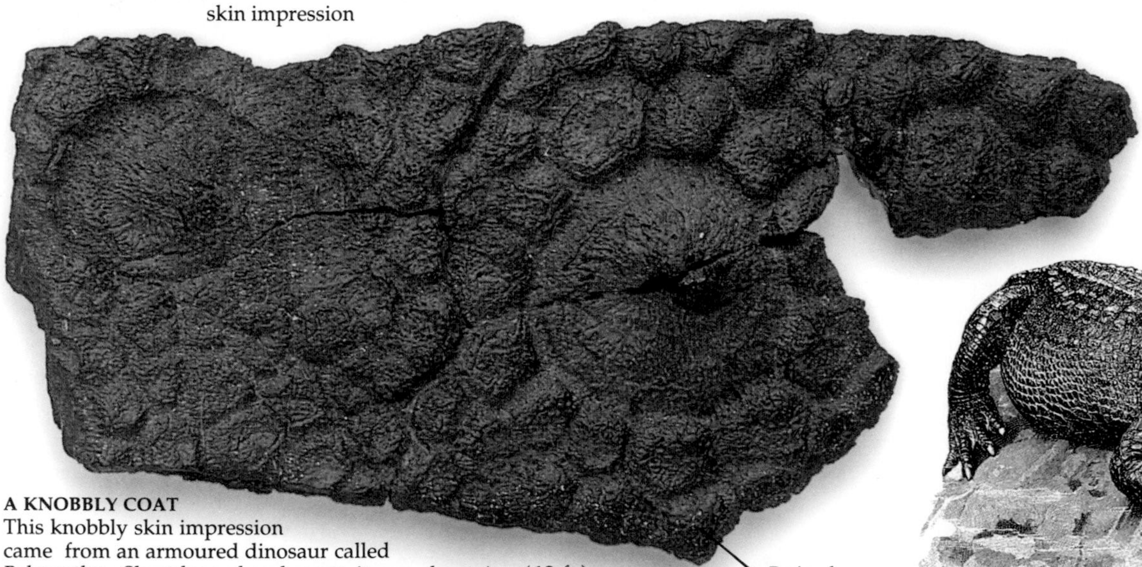

A KNOBBLY COAT
This knobbly skin impression came from an armoured dinosaur called *Polacanthus*. Short-legged and squat, it was about 4 m (13 ft) long, and had sharp spines running along its back. These, combined with its overlapping bony plates, would have discouraged hungry meat eaters from attacking.

Raised nodules for protection

LIKE A CROCODILE?
Crocodiles, being reptiles, have the same type of skin as the dinosaurs - ideally adapted to conditions on dry land. The knobbly skin on this "smiling" crocodile is like the *Polacanthus* impression (left).

Central ridge of nodule

The ankylosaurs had bones which were fused together to form a bony armour. The armoured "tanks" of the dinosaur world, these creatures were squat and very heavy. They looked rather like giant reptilian armadillos. They had small jaws and weak teeth, and ate plants. They protected themselves from large carnivores mainly by crouching and clinging to the ground, relying completely on their tough skins for defence.

THE COMPLETE BEAST
This is what *Edmontonia*, one of the largest ankylosaurs, probably looked like when it was alive. Its armour included spikes that guarded its shoulders and flanks from attack, and rows of bony plates.

Smaller scales for flexibility

ANKYLOSAUR NODULE
Many ankylosaur nodules looked like this one. The flattened base was attached to the creature's back, and the broad central ridge provided protection. In life, it was covered by a horny scale (like a fingernail). In the picture, it is possible to make out the pitted areas where this was attached.

Sauropod skin impression

Bigger scales where skin did not have to bend

UNARMOURED AND SCALY
Quite smooth compared to the ankylosaurs, this skin impression came from a sauropod dinosaur, probably one like *Diplodocus* (pp. 14-21). The skin was scaly, not bony like the ankylosaurs, and would have given little protection against attack. The scales, although packed tightly together, had flexible edges where they touched, acting like "hinges" to allow easy movement. You can see from this impression that the scales varied in size, the smaller ones occurring where the skin had to bend a lot.

Plated dinosaurs

ONE OF THE MOST unusual groups of dinosaurs were the stegosaurs, named after the North American dinosaur, *Stegosaurus*. Easily recognized by the double row of plates running down their backs, stegosaurs also had sharp spikes on the ends of their tails, used for lashing out in defence. Despite their fearsome appearance, these dinosaurs were all plant eaters. They usually walked on all-fours, browsing on low vegetation - a way of feeding which suited their low-slung heads perfectly. Their small weak teeth could only handle soft plants. The word "stegosaur" actually means "roof lizard", because it was once thought that the plates lay flat on the dinosaur's back, like tiles on a roof. Although this arrangement would have provided slightly better protection against attack from carnosaurs, it is more likely that the plates stood upright in two rows along the stegosaur's back. Some people think that the plates were fixed to the skeleton, but they were actually embedded in the dinosaur's thick skin.

THE PLATE DEBATE
Scientists have long argued about how *Stegosaurus'* plates were arranged. Here they are alternated, but they are often shown in paired rows. The plates were made of bone with honeycomb-like spaces running through - not much use as defensive armour plating.

A WEIRD STEGOSAUR
This etching shows an early attempt to reconstruct a plated dinosaur - with hedgehog-like spines instead of bony plates! However, there is evidence from hip bone fossils that one stegosaur at least, *Stegosaurus*, could have reared up on its hind legs like this.

Vertebral spine

Cone-shaped plate

Chevron bone

A STING IN THE TAIL
The large, cone-shaped plates on the back of *Tuojiangosaurus* give way to two pairs of sharply pointed ones, which were used as lethal weapons. Stegosaurs could swing their muscular tails from side to side with great force.

Broad, flat feet

Sharp defensive spike

WARMING UP

Dimetrodon was an early reptile that lived before the dinosaurs. It used the large sail on its back to absorb the heat of the sun on cool days, and so warm its body. Some plated dinosaurs did the same.

Some stegosaurs made use of solar power

Stegosaurus plate

CLOSE-UP PLATE

Shown at half life-size, this is one of the smaller plates from the neck region of *Stegosaurus*. These large, flat bones acted like the sail of *Dimetrodon* (above left) to warm or cool the animal. The plates were richly supplied with blood, and *Stegosaurus* would have used this blood like water in a central-heating system. Standing in the breeze would have cooled the blood, while basking in the sun would have raised its temperature, thereby warming the dinosaur.

The Chinese stegosaur, *Tuojiangosaurus*

Small narrow head with walnut-sized brain

POORLY DEFENDED

Like all stegosaurs, *Tuojiangosaurus'* flanks and belly were vulnerable to attack. The spikes in the tail were the main weapon used to fend off attacks of large meat-eating dinosaurs.

Long hind limbs

Short front limbs

PEA BRAIN

Stegosaurs are famous for having tiny brains in proportion to their size. *Stegosaurus* had a brain the size of a walnut. This has given some people the idea that dinosaurs were stupid or slow. But stegosaurs' brains were obviously ample for their needs, as they managed to survive for over 10 million years.

Fast movers

NOT ALL DINOSAURS WERE HUGE and lumbering. Some were built for speed, either to flee attackers, or to pursue prey. Unlike fast-running living animals like horses, which are all four-footed, fast-moving dinosaurs ran on their hind legs alone. As a result, all the fast movers looked quite similar. They all tended to have long back legs, in order to take long strides. Slender legs and narrow feet can be moved quickly and so allowed the dinosaurs to run more efficiently. The rest of the body was usually light and fairly short, balanced by a slender tail. The arms were lightly built, with small-clawed hands, and the neck was long, with a small head on the top. Some of the nimble dinosaurs could reach speeds of 56 kph (35 mph) - almost as fast as a racehorse. They could take advantage of their speed in two ways: either to pursue a victim, or to beat a hasty retreat from an attacker. Herbivorous and carnivorous fast-moving dinosaurs were involved in a kind of "race": plant eaters evolved faster and faster types in order to avoid being caught by ever-improving meat eaters.

OSTRICH LOOKALIKE
Struthiomimus, or "ostrich mimic", looked remarkably like an ostrich, and probably ran in a very similar way. Scientists even think it probably had feathers. The main difference is *Struthiomimus*' long bony tail, and its clawed hands in place of wings.

TINY AND TOOTHY
This fast-moving dinosaur, *Heterodontosaurus*, was only about 1 m (3 ft) long. It had three different types of teeth, but was still a herbivore.

Long neck was stretched forward as Gallimimus ran

Gallimimus in motion

Stiffened tail for balancing

A POOR GRIP
Closely related to *Struthiomimus* (above left) *Gallimimus* was remarkably bird-like with its toothless beak. Its hands were not adapted for grasping things.

SPRINTING DINOSAURS
Small, agile plant-eating dinosaurs like *Hypsilophodon* (below) were among the fastest runners. By measuring their legs and comparing their shape to those of modern animals, experts have estimated that they reached speeds of 45 kph (30 mph).

Narrow feet for speed

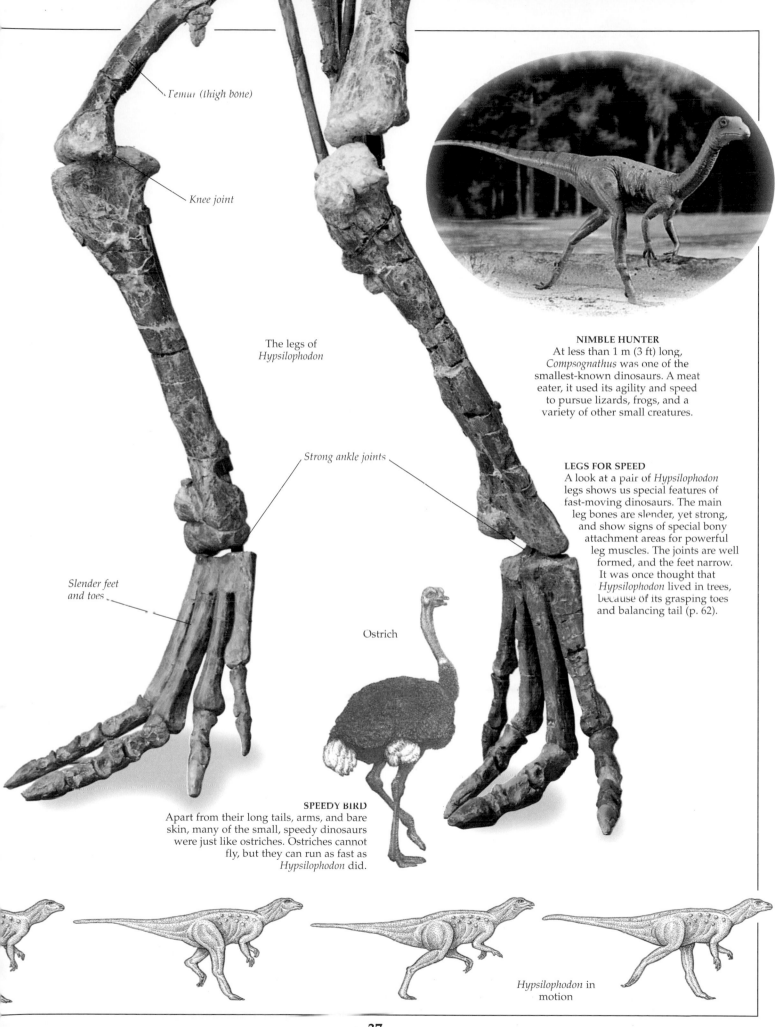

Femur (thigh bone)

Knee joint

The legs of
Hypsilophodon

Strong ankle joints

Slender feet
and toes

Ostrich

NIMBLE HUNTER
At less than 1 m (3 ft) long,
Compsognathus was one of the
smallest-known dinosaurs. A meat
eater, it used its agility and speed
to pursue lizards, frogs, and a
variety of other small creatures.

LEGS FOR SPEED
A look at a pair of *Hypsilophodon*
legs shows us special features of
fast-moving dinosaurs. The main
leg bones are slender, yet strong,
and show signs of special bony
attachment areas for powerful
leg muscles. The joints are well
formed, and the feet narrow.
It was once thought that
Hypsilophodon lived in trees,
because of its grasping toes
and balancing tail (p. 62).

SPEEDY BIRD
Apart from their long tails, arms, and bare
skin, many of the small, speedy dinosaurs
were just like ostriches. Ostriches cannot
fly, but they can run as fast as
Hypsilophodon did.

Hypsilophodon in
motion

37

Two feet or four?

WHY DID SOME DINOSAURS WALK on four legs, while others walked on two? The answer is simple – dinosaurs walked in the way that suited their lifestyle best. Most carnivores, for instance, walked on their hind legs, because they needed to use their hands to catch and hold on to their prey. Other dinosaurs usually walked on all four legs, mainly because their enormous size and weight needed support from four sturdy "posts" underneath. However, fossil finds suggest that even a large, heavy herbivore such as *Diplodocus* (p. 14) was able to rear up on its hind legs – for short periods, at least. Some dinosaurs, for example hadrosaurs, had the option of walking either on two or four legs, depending on what they were doing at the time. Mostly, it suited them to move around slowly on all-fours, so that they could browse on low-growing vegetation. When they were alarmed, however, they could rear up and charge off on hind legs alone. These dinosaurs needed special "hands" that allowed for weight support, as well as grasping.

A sauropod mother rears to defend its young

"DON'T COME ANY NEARER!"
This museum model shows a mother *Barosaurus* rearing up on its two hind legs. It is defending its young against an attack by an *Allosaurus*. However, scientists are still debating whether a huge sauropod would – or could – have behaved like this.

HANDY SUPPORT
This hadrosaur toe bone from the "hand" is typically flattened and slightly hoof-like. It could support the dinosaur's weight when it was grazing on all-fours.

Hadrosaur toe

FOUR-LEGGED TOE
Triceratops always walked on four legs, so this *Triceratops* toe bone could come from either the front or back foot. The toe bone is broader and more hoof-like than the hadrosaur one (above). That is because the hadrosaur did not use its front feet so much.

Triceratops toe

Hoof-like claw

Scelidosaurus foot

Ankle bones

SOMETHING AFOOT?
This is the complete hind foot of an early plant-eating dinosaur called *Scelidosaurus*. It was heavily armoured with bony, jaw-breaking studs which ran the length of its body. *Scelidosaurus* always walked on four legs, and its hind foot was strong and broad, with four powerful toes to support the heavy body. The small first toe would have barely reached the ground.

HAND OR FOOT?

We know this is a hand because of the sharp, narrow claws used for holding things, or tearing leaves off trees. It came from *Plateosaurus*, a plant eater that fed on plants at ground level (on all-fours), and then reared up on its hind legs to reach the treetops. The joints between the bones allowed the hand to be bent back to allow *Plateosaurus* to walk on all-fours.

First toe

Narrow, sharp claw

FEEBLE HANDS

The mighty *Tyrannosaurus rex* had surprisingly small hands in proportion to its body, with only two claws. They were too short to hold prey, but they may have been used as anchors to grip the ground when *Tyrannosaurus rex* rose from resting.

Toes ending in hooves

Fourth finger

Second finger

Iguanodon hand

Thumb spike

Flexible fifth finger

SPIKY CUSTOMER

Although *Iguanodon* was most often pictured on two legs wielding its thumb spike (right), it actually spent much of its time on all-fours.

MULTI-PURPOSE HAND

Iguanodon's hand is remarkable because it shows clearly the different uses to which a hand can be put. The large thumb spike was used as a fearsome defensive weapon. The middle three fingers, which ended in hoof-like bones, were used exclusively for walking on, and the fifth finger was flexible, and used for holding food.

Wrist bones

Ancient footprints

As WELL AS LEAVING their fossilized bones as evidence, dinosaurs also made their mark on the Earth in the form of footprints. Tracks have been found where dinosaurs walked in soft, swampy land, for example along riverbanks, in search of food and water. Later on, the prints would have dried and hardened in the sun. Eventually, through rain or flooding, water would have brought more sand or mud which buried the prints until they gradually fossilized. Called trace fossils, because they are not actually a part of an animal, these footprints can tell us much about how dinosaurs moved. A lot of the same types of prints found together, for instance, with smaller ones in the middle, suggests that some dinosaurs moved in herds, with the young ones protected in the centre.

RUNNING ALL OVER THE WORLD
Dinosaur trackways have been found all over the world. These tracks found in Queensland, Australia, came from small meat eaters, running together as a pack. Experts can judge the speed at which they were moving by measuring the distance between the prints.

Toe bone

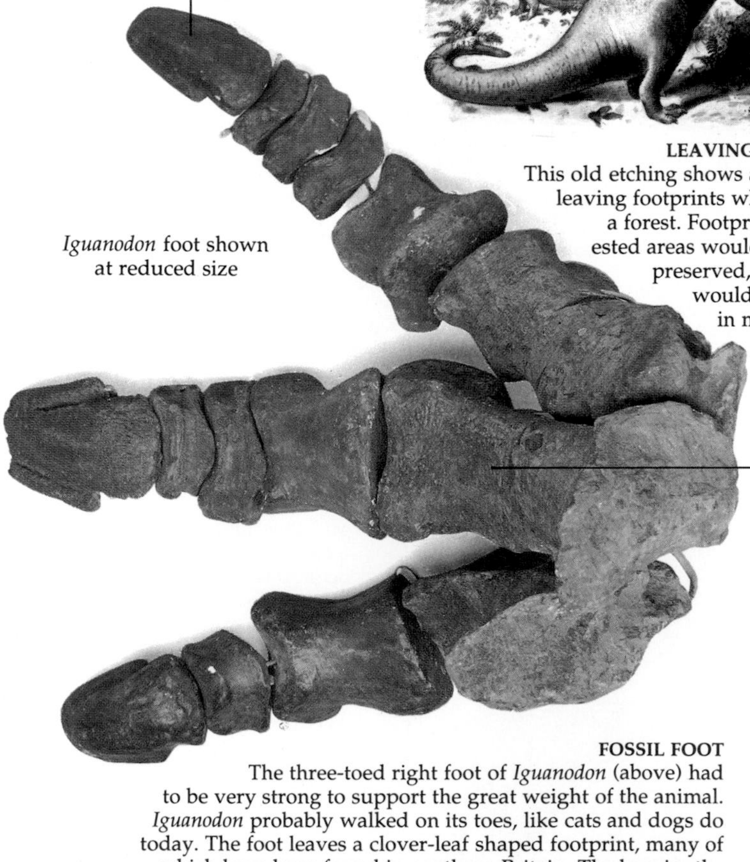

Iguanodon foot shown at reduced size

LEAVING EVIDENCE?
This old etching shows an *Iguanodon* leaving footprints while feeding in a forest. Footprints left in forested areas would not have been preserved, however - they would need to be made in more swampy land.

Upper foot bone

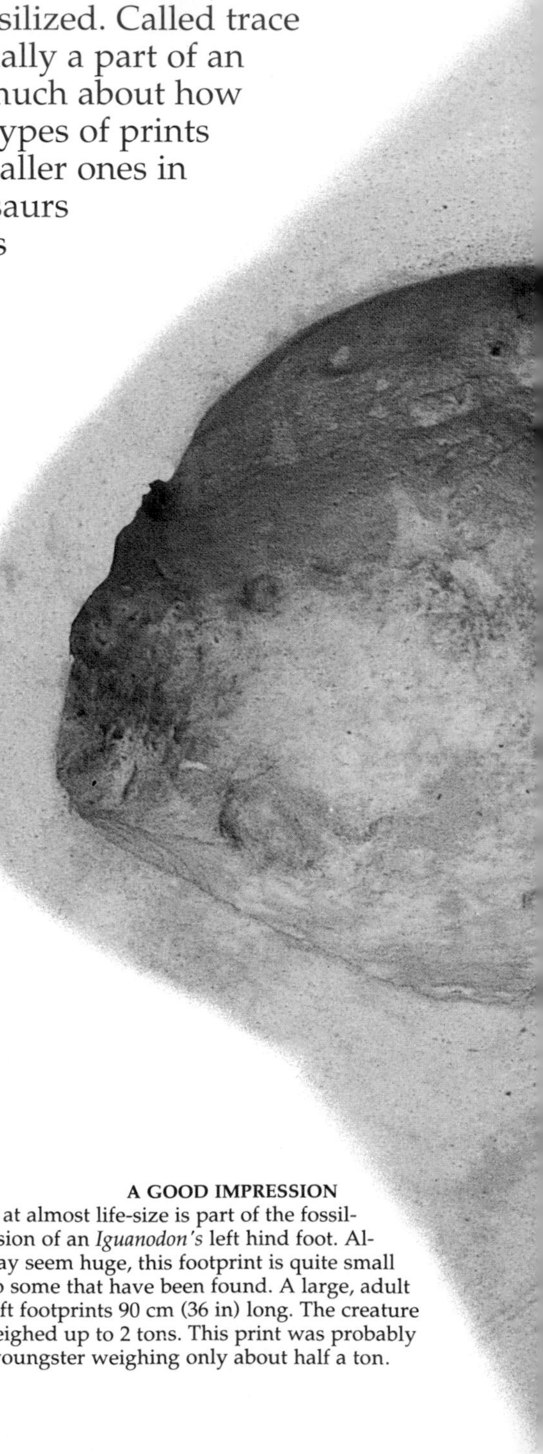

A GOOD IMPRESSION
Shown here at almost life-size is part of the fossilized impression of an *Iguanodon's* left hind foot. Although it may seem huge, this footprint is quite small compared to some that have been found. A large, adult *Iguanodon* left footprints 90 cm (36 in) long. The creature probably weighed up to 2 tons. This print was probably made by a youngster weighing only about half a ton.

FOSSIL FOOT
The three-toed right foot of *Iguanodon* (above) had to be very strong to support the great weight of the animal. *Iguanodon* probably walked on its toes, like cats and dogs do today. The foot leaves a clover-leaf shaped footprint, many of which have been found in southern Britain. The heavier the dinosaur, the better the footprint (right).

Iguanodon footprint

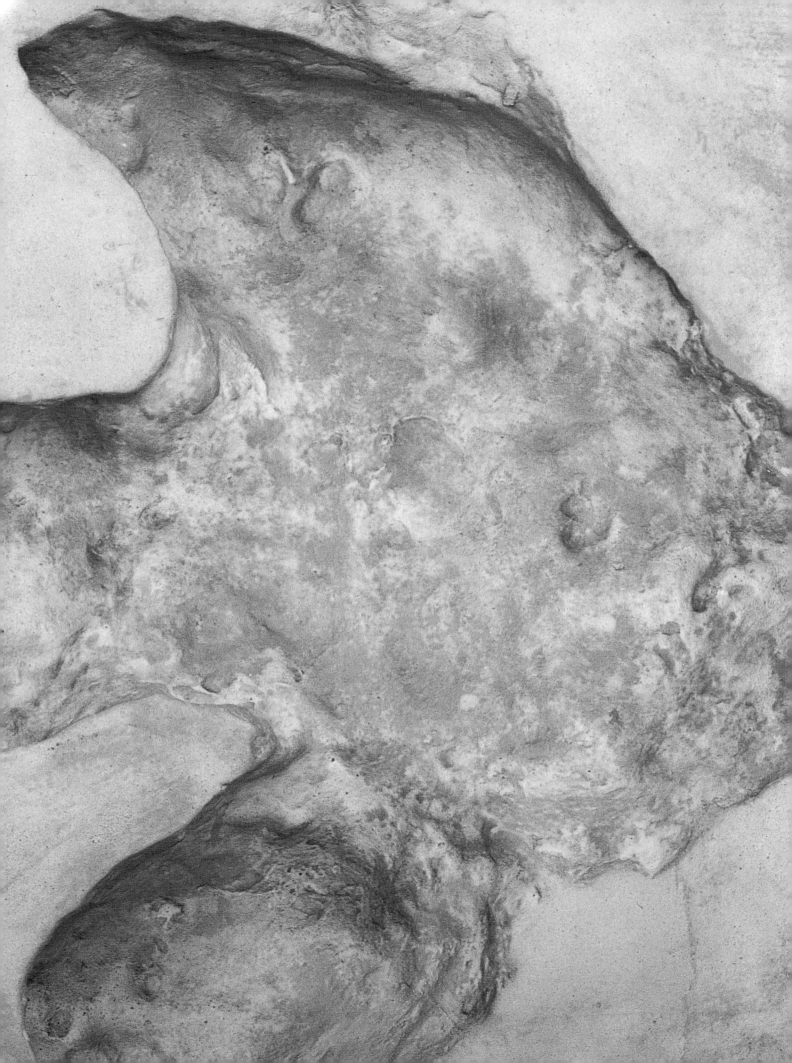

Claws and their uses

CLAW BONES ALL HAVE stories to tell about the lifestyle of their owners. Dinosaurs that hunted and killed other animals tended to have very narrow, sharp, curved claws, like the talons on the foot of an eagle. They used their claws like daggers, to gain a secure hold and to stop their unfortunate victim from escaping. The claws also helped to injure, or even kill, the prey. Perhaps the most terrifying clawed predator of the dinosaur age was *Deinonychus*, or "terrible claw". It had a huge sickle-like claw on its second toe, and long arms with three-fingered clawed hands. It would leap on its victim, slashing with its claws, and using its long tail to balance. Plant-eating and omnivorous dinosaurs, by contrast, did not have such sharp, talon-like claws. They tended to be broader and more flattened, as they did not need to kill. They were also stronger and more rugged because they were often put to many uses, from walking, to scraping or digging for food. Sometimes these hoof-like claws were used in defence, as crude weapons to slash out at attacking meat eaters.

Tubercle (swelling) for strong muscle attachment

THUMB CLAW
This smallish claw came from the thumb of *Massospondylus*. The slight swelling at the base was where a strong muscle was attached.

"LEAPING LIZARDS"
Caught in action, with their teeth bared, these sparring meat eaters show how they best used their claws - for vicious attack!

CREEPY CLAWS
This feathered dinosaur is *Velociraptor*, or "quick robber". Its jaws were lined with razor-sharp teeth, but its most formidable weapons were four sets of deadly, hooked claws. Using its hand to hold on to its prey, *Velociraptor* would have been agile enough to raise a clawed foot and deliver a killer kick, slashing through its victim's flesh.

Flattened claw

NOT FOR ATTACK
This claw belongs to *Ornithomimus*. Although this dinosaur was a meat eater, its claws were quite flattened, and would not have been much use for defence or attack.

FISHING TACKLE
This hand claw was found in 1983 in
southern England, along with other remains
the skeleton. It was named *Baryonyx*,
meaning "heavy claw". The dinosaur
belongs to an unusual group of
dinosaurs also known from Africa
(pp. 54-55). A flesh eater, it
may have used its highly
curved claw like a
harpoon, to catch fish
for its dinner!

ELEPHANT FEET
This huge claw came from a relative of *Diplodocus*
(pp. 14-21), called *Apatosaurus*. A plant eater, it
walked on four, pillar-like legs and had rounded
feet, like an elephant's. Most of its claws were
short and hoof-like, except for the inside one
on the front foot, shown here. This claw
may have been used for digging, or
even for defence.

Groove where horny
covering was attached
to claw

Rough bone for
attachment of heavy
claw horn

Baryonyx
claw

SUPER SCYTHES
Therizinosaurus (left) was one of the so-called
"scythe lizards". Its outsize claws look deadly,
but they would have made awkward weapons.
Perhaps they were used to rake up plants, slit
open termites' nests – or even just for display.

Eggs and nests

A baby *Maiasaura* (p. 46) emerges from its egg

Dinosaurs, like reptiles and birds today, laid hard-shelled eggs. We know this because many fossilized dinosaur eggs have been found, some even containing small skeletons. Sometimes the eggs have been found in nests, with remains of the parent dinosaurs nearby. Nests found complete with fossilized young tell us that baby dinosaurs, like baby birds, would instinctively stay in their nest, no matter what happened to their mother. Several nests found close together suggest that some dinosaurs nested in colonies. It is perhaps surprising that dinosaur eggs were never very huge. If they were in proportion to the size of some adult dinosaurs, the shells would have been far too thick to hatch, and would not have allowed enough oxygen to reach the creatures growing inside.

Cracks which occurred during fossilization

Oviraptor egg

Unidentified dinosaur egg

Quail egg

DINOSAUR AND BIRD
The hatchling that would have emerged from the dinosaur egg (right) would have had lots of growing to do before it was an adult – far more than a chick from a modern bird's egg, such as the quail egg (above).

Textured dinosaur eggshell

GROUND NESTER
This model shows an *Oviraptor* mother brooding its clutch of eggs. Its nest is scraped into a mound, a design that would have stopped the eggs from rolling away and also given some shelter. Like many ground-nesting birds today, *Oviraptor* may have used her body heat to incubate the eggs until they hatched.

A HARD SHELL
This elongated egg was part of the first evidence that dinosaurs laid eggs. They laid their eggs on land, just like lizards do today. The amphibians, from which they evolved, had to lay their eggs in water, where they hatched into tadpoles. Reptiles, however, can lay their eggs on land because the eggs have tough shells with a private pond inside for the young to develop safely. Laying eggs like this was probably one of the reasons why the dinosaurs survived on Earth for so long.

THE EGG THIEF?

In the 1920s this fossilized nest, and many more like it, was discovered in the Gobi Desert of Mongolia and China. For a long time, scientists believed the nests belonged to the horned, plant eating dinosaur, *Protoceratops*. When remains of an *Oviraptor* were found on the fossil site, it was thought to have been there as a scavenger, stealing the eggs - the name *Oviraptor* means "egg thief". Gradually, however, more and more *Oviraptor* remains were found. In the 1990s scientists finally realized that the nests and eggs belonged to *Oviraptor*, not *Protoceratops*.

Nest in which eggs were buried has turned into sandstone through fossilization process

Birth and growth

BECAUSE MOST OF the dinosaurs were so big, it is hard to imagine them as going through baby and juvenile, as well as adult stages in their lives. But recent discoveries have enabled us to piece together a little of their early lives. We know that dinosaur mothers laid their eggs in hollowed-out nests in the ground (pp. 44-45). In some cases, tiny skeletons of hatchlings have been found inside the eggs. Colonies of duckbill dinosaur nests have been found containing skeletons of hatchlings. Their teeth are worn, indicating that the mother dinosaur would have brought food back to the nest. Baby dinosaurs probably grew fast. In the case of sauropods, which moved in herds (p. 12), the youngsters probably walked in the middle, protected by the adults on the outside. Some dinosaurs, like the ceratopians, changed their bodily proportions as they grew up.

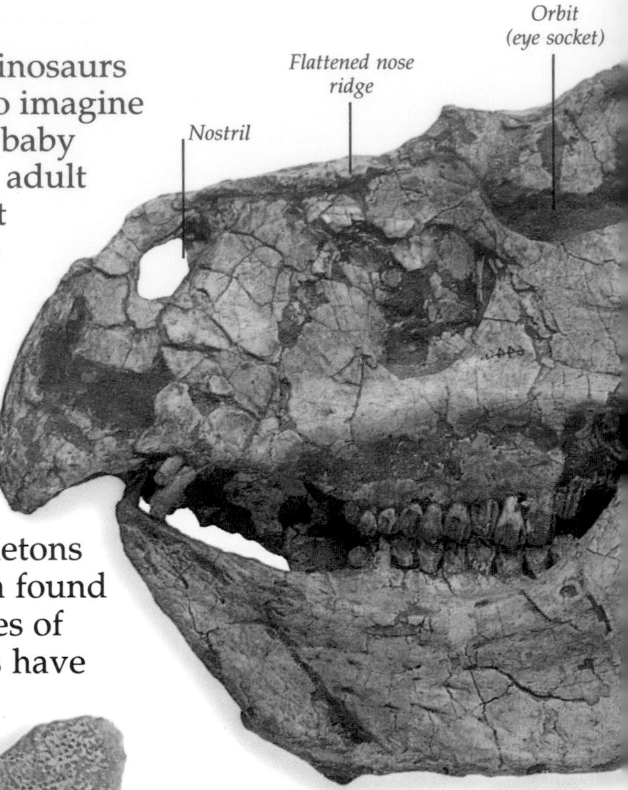

THE NURSERY
This old illustration was drawn when the Gobi Desert eggs were thought to be *Protoceratops'*. It shows how people imagined a dinosaur nursery. There are baby *Protoceratops* at various stages - some hatching, some taking their first steps, some struggling to get out of the sand!

Flattened nose ridge

Nostril

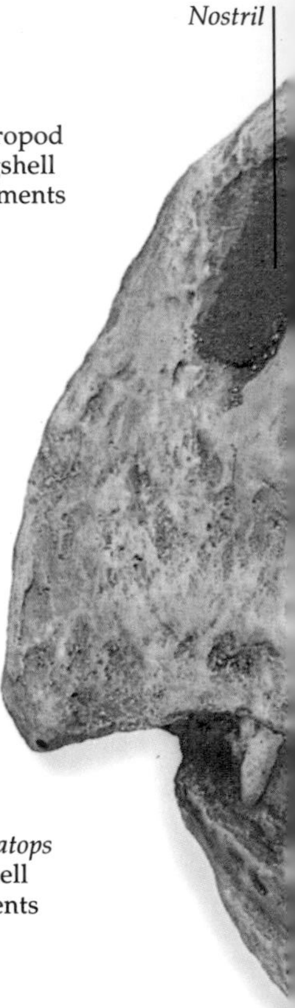

Orbit (eye socket)

Nostril

Sauropod eggshell fragments

GIANT SHELLS
These fragments come from large round eggs that were laid by huge sauropod dinosaurs like *Diplodocus* (p. 14).

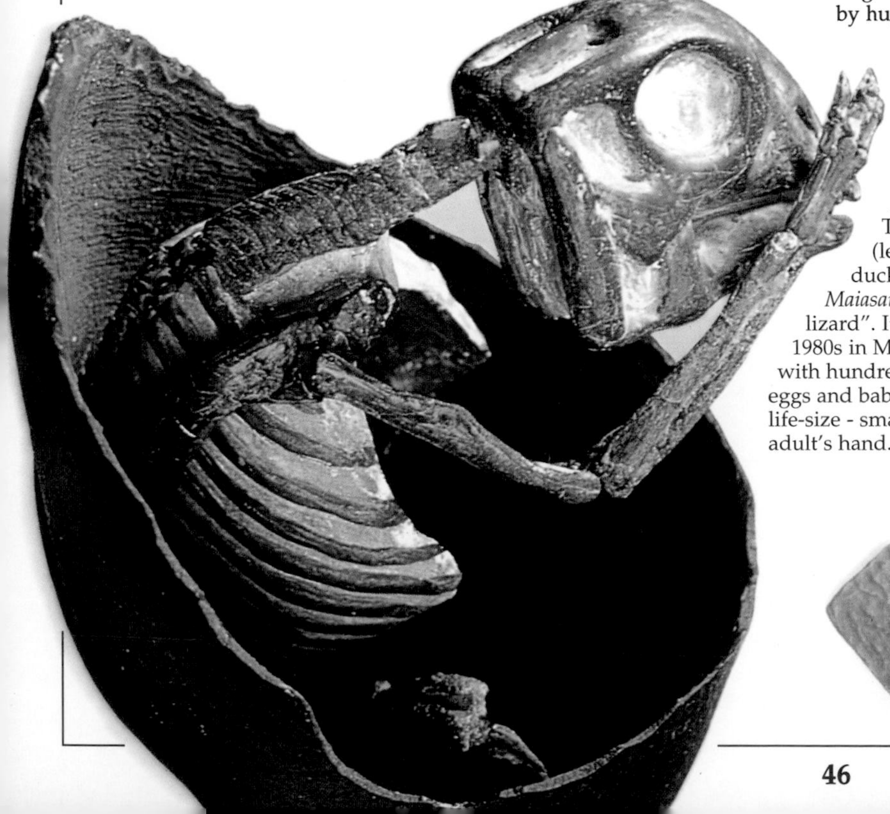

A BEAST EMERGES
This fossilized eggshell (left) contains a hatching duckbill dinosaur called *Maiasaura*, or "good mother lizard". It was found in the 1980s in Montana, USA, along with hundreds of other dinosaur eggs and babies. It is shown here at life-size - small enough to fit in an adult's hand.

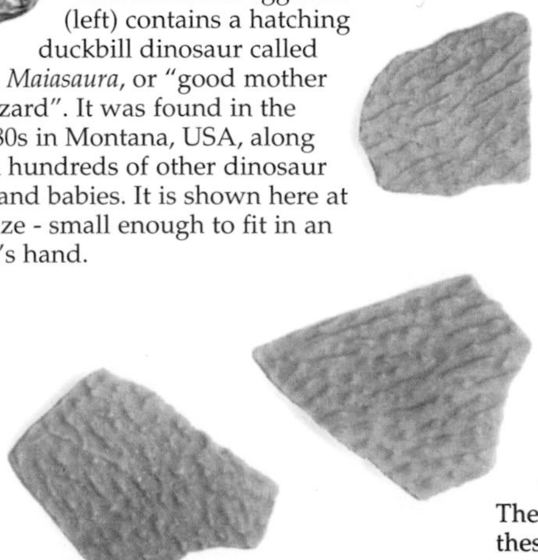

Protoceratops eggshell fragments

COARSE SHELLS
The coarse, pimply surface of these *Protoceratops* shell fragments is typical of many dinosaur eggs.

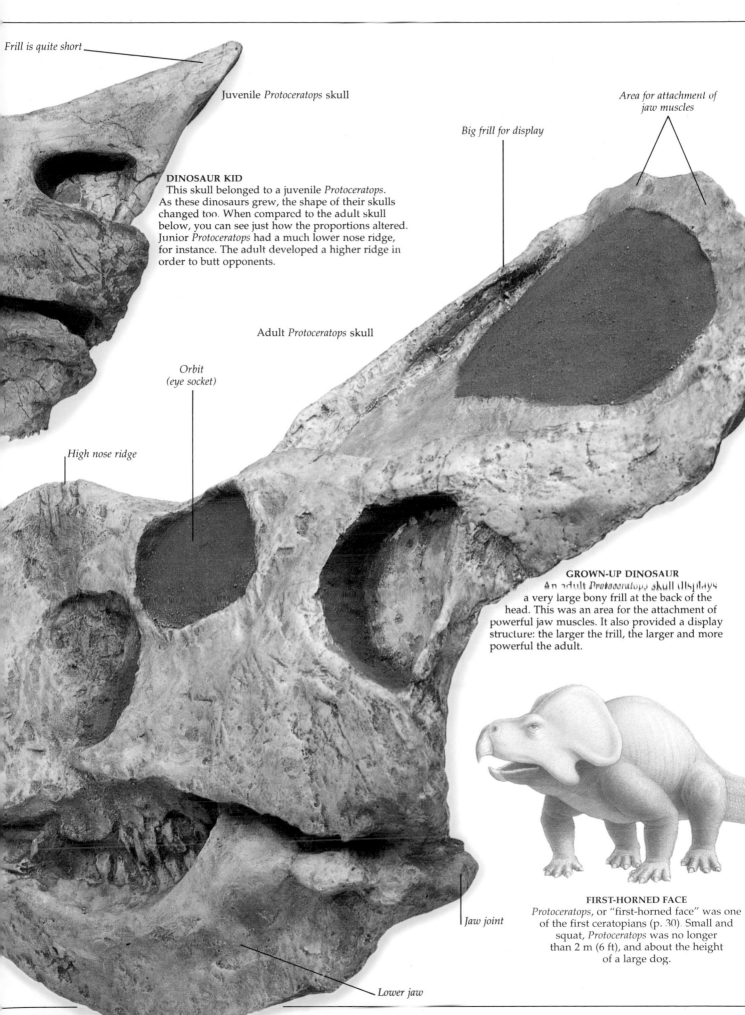

Frill is quite short

Juvenile *Protoceratops* skull

Area for attachment of
jaw muscles

Big frill for display

DINOSAUR KID
This skull belonged to a juvenile *Protoceratops*.
As these dinosaurs grew, the shape of their skulls
changed too. When compared to the adult skull
below, you can see just how the proportions altered.
Junior *Protoceratops* had a much lower nose ridge,
for instance. The adult developed a higher ridge in
order to butt opponents.

Adult *Protoceratops* skull

Orbit
(eye socket)

High nose ridge

GROWN-UP DINOSAUR
An adult *Protoceratops* skull displays
a very large bony frill at the back of the
head. This was an area for the attachment of
powerful jaw muscles. It also provided a display
structure: the larger the frill, the larger and more
powerful the adult.

Jaw joint

Lower jaw

FIRST-HORNED FACE
Protoceratops, or "first-horned face" was one
of the first ceratopians (p. 30). Small and
squat, *Protoceratops* was no longer
than 2 m (6 ft), and about the height
of a large dog.

47

Death of the dinosaurs

DINOSAURS DISAPPEARED from the Earth quite suddenly, and why this happened is still a mystery. Around 70 million years ago, the dinosaurs ruled the Earth. Yet about five million years later, they had all died out, perhaps only in a matter of months. Various theories have been put forward to explain their sudden extinction, including that small mammals ate all the dinosaur eggs. But this and other theories often ignore one vital point: a whole range of creatures died out at the same time as the dinosaurs, including all the swimming and flying reptiles. So any theory to explain dinosaur extinction must account for the disappearance of these groups as well. The most likely explanation seems to be that the Earth experienced a cataclysmic event - a meteorite impact, and possibly also tremendous volcanic eruptions - which caused global environmental destruction.

POISONOUS BITE
It has been suggested that dinosaurs died out because they ate new kinds of poisonous plants, such as deadly nightshade, that started-growing on the Earth. However, this theory does not explain why other creatures, such as marine reptiles, died out as well.

Stony meteorite fragment

ROCKS FROM SPACE
A massive meteorite strike would have had catastrophic consequences. The impact would have thrown a huge cloud of hot gas and debris into the atmosphere, darkening the Earth for a long time. With no sunlight, plants would not have been able to grow, and the animals that fed on them would have died.

A MASS EXTINCTION
Many other creatures died out at the time of the dinosaur extinction. Whatever happened seemed to affect some creatures, but left others unscathed. Ammonites (left), a type of shellfish, became extinct, as did the mosasaurs, plesiosaurs, and ichthyosaurs, groups of meat-eating marine reptiles (below). Sea crocodiles died out but the river crocodiles survived. The flying reptiles, pterosaurs, disappeared, but birds were unaffected.

Fossilized ammonite

Iron meteorite fragment

The biggest teeth were 25 cm (10 in) long, but much of this was embedded in the jaw

Kronosaurus (a plesiosaur)

Massive muscles moved the flippers up and down, propelling the animal through the water

VOLCANIC WINTER

The end of the dinosaurs also coincided with a period of extreme volcanic activity. Massive volcanic eruptions occurred in what is now Central India, pouring forth enormous lava flows and blasting vast amounts of dust and gas high into the atmosphere. Blown around the world by winds, the dust may have blotted out the Sun and caused a fundamental climate change that devastated the planet's ecosystems.

IMPACT EVIDENCE

In 1990, a huge meteorite crater 180 km (110 miles) across was discovered on the seabed off the coast of Yucatán, Mexico. The meteorite, some 10 km (6 miles) across, struck the Earth at about 100,000 kph (62,000 mph). Dating from about 65 million years ago, this colossal impact probably triggered the mass extinction that killed off the dinosaurs.

Dinosaur or bird?

Are birds the descendants of the dinosaurs? The debate first began with the discovery of a fossil bird, *Archaeopteryx*. It lived 150 million years ago, alongside the dinosaurs. It had feathers, like all birds, but also reptilian features, such as teeth. Could this be the missing link between dinosaurs and birds? *Archaeopteryx* was shown to share over 20 features with meat-eating dinosaurs such as *Coelophysis*, right. One gap in the evidence was the lack of any dinosaur fossils with a wishbone: birds have a well-developed one that helps to keep the wing joint in position. But now we know that several dinosaurs - mainly meat eaters - did have a wishbone. More dramatically, fossil hunters in China have unearthed feather traces belonging to bird-like dinosaurs such as *Sinosauropteryx*, *Caudipteryx*, and *Sinornithosaurus*. Some scientists also think theropods in North America, including *Bambiraptor* and *Troodon*, were feathered.

BIRDS OF A FEATHER
Archaeopteryx, seen here preening on a branch (pp. 10-11), had several un-bird-like features. It had a long tail with bones down the middle, claws on its wings, and teeth. Its wings were designed for flight, but it is unlikely that *Archaeopteryx* could have flown as well as modern birds.

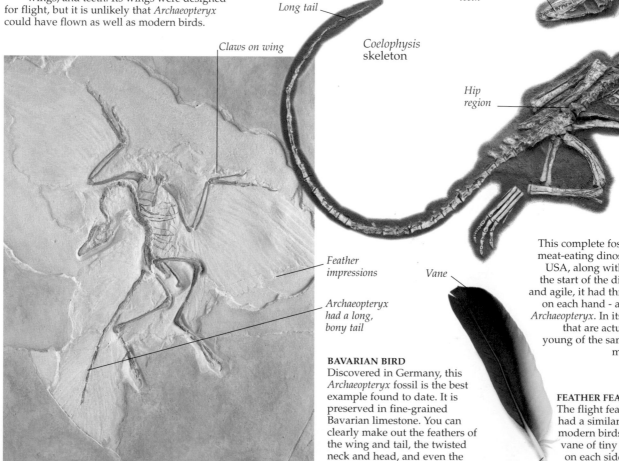

Long tail

Claws on wing

Sharp, predatory teeth

Coelophysis skeleton

Hip region

Remains of young *Coelophysis* in belly

Feather impressions

Archaeopteryx had a long, bony tail

Vane

BAVARIAN BIRD
Discovered in Germany, this *Archaeopteryx* fossil is the best example found to date. It is preserved in fine-grained Bavarian limestone. You can clearly make out the feathers of the wing and tail, the twisted neck and head, and even the claws on its wings.

Shaft

FOSSIL FABLE
This complete fossil of *Coelophysis*, a small meat-eating dinosaur, was found in Texas, USA, along with many others. It lived at the start of the dinosaur age. Lightly built and agile, it had three strong clawed fingers on each hand - a feature in common with *Archaeopteryx*. In its belly you can see bones that are actually the remains of some young of the same species. So *Coelophysis* may have been a cannibal.

FEATHER FEATURES
The flight feathers of *Archaeopteryx* had a similar structure to those of modern birds, with a shaft and a vane of tiny branches called barbs on each side. The barbs hooked together to form the feather surface.

Bambiraptor

A wrist joint like a bird's would have enabled Bambiraptor *to fold its hands as a bird folds its wings*

BAMBI'S BONES
Bambiraptor had a wishbone and some of its bones had air sacs, just like the bones of a bird. The dinosaur also had large eye sockets and a bigger brain cavity for its size than any other dinosaur. However, its deep snout and large teeth were not at all bird-like.

Bambiraptor skeleton

BAMBIRAPTOR IN ACTION
A bird-like dinosaur called *Bambiraptor* was discovered in Montana in 1994. It could not fly, but must have been a fast runner, able to hunt frogs and small mammals. It was probably covered with downy feathers that kept in its body heat.

Downy fluff covered much of Sinornithosaurus's *body*

FLAPPING HUNTER
Sinornithosaurus was a dromaeosaurid - a small, agile hunter with large eyes, sharp teeth, and a distinctive sickle-shaped toe claw. It was one of the first dinosaurs discovered with a bird-like shoulder girdle, suggesting that it could flap its arms.

Long arm feathers

Brightly coloured short tail

Sinosauropteryx

IMPORTANT FIND
In 1996, the discovery of *Sinosauropteryx* changed the way people thought about dinosaurs. Its fossils revealed that its back and tail were covered in a coat of feather-like filaments, showing that not all dinosaurs had scaly skin.

COLOURFUL CHARACTER?
Caudipteryx was a turkey-sized dinosaur discovered in China. Its teeth and bones, especially its forward-pointing pubic bone, indicate that *Caudipteryx* was a dinosaur. However, it had a beak, feathers, and short tail. As with other feathered dinosaurs, no one knows what colour *Caudipteryx*'s feathers were. They may have been brightly coloured and used for spectacular mating displays, as well as keeping the dinosaur warm.

How to find a dinosaur

HOW DO SCIENTISTS go about discovering dinosaur remains? Because the dinosaurs became fossilized in the first place by being buried in sand, or mud, we know that their fossils can only be found in sedimentary rock - rock that has been built up in layers over the years. Fossils are often found by accident, by builders, or quarrymen digging into the ground. Fossil collectors may set out deliberately to search an area that is thought to be rich in fossils. Sometimes a large and highly organized scientific expedition is undertaken, based on detailed research. Whatever the method of discovery, careful preparation must be done if the find is to be recovered successfully. Records need to be made of the exact position of the find, and the right tools are needed to ensure that the fossils are extracted from the site and returned to the laboratory without being damaged.

THE FIND!
Discoveries of fossil dinosaurs are rare, and best tackled by a team of experienced people.

DUTCH DISCOVERY
The jaws of the mighty sea lizard *Mosasaurus* were discovered deep in a chalk mine near Maastricht in Holland in 1770. This etching shows the team of discoverers working by torchlight.

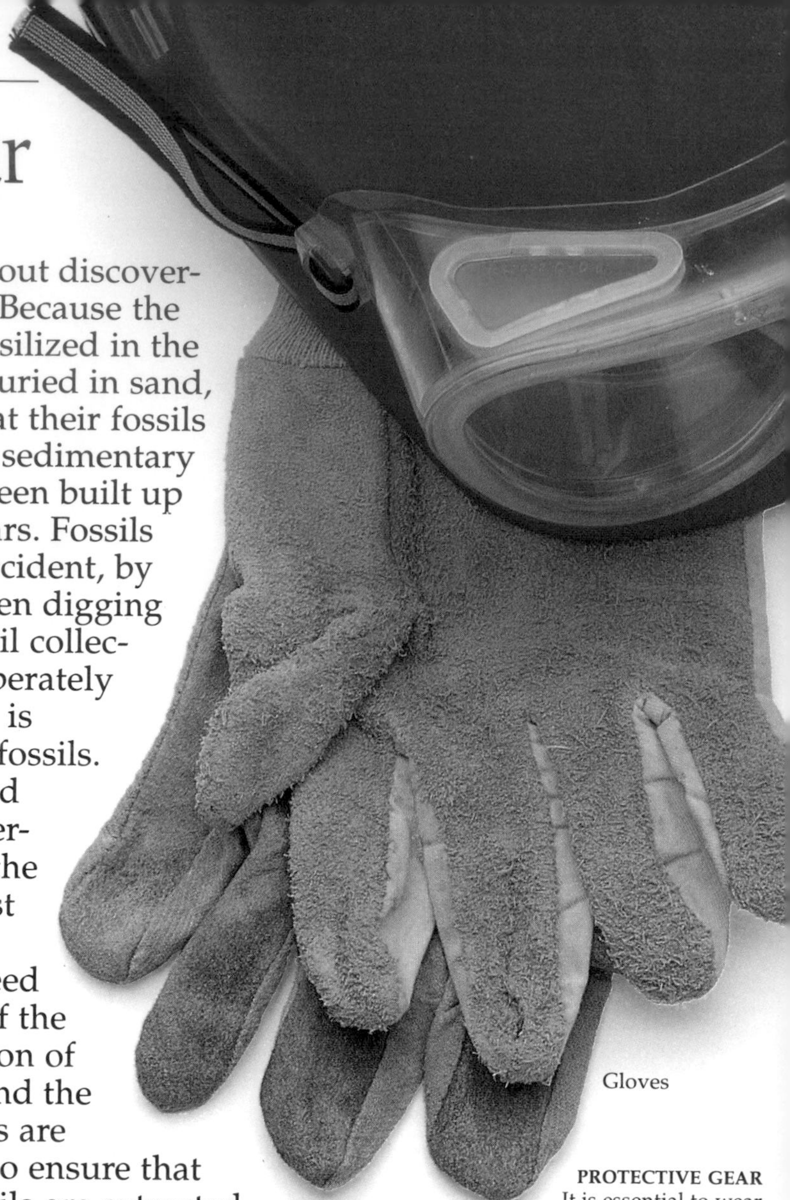

Gloves

PROTECTIVE GEAR
It is essential to wear proper protective clothing while on a fossil dig. Gloves are needed where heavy hammering and chiselling is to be done, as are goggles to prevent splinters of rock from damaging the eyes. A hard hat is also advisable, especially if work is being done near cliffs.

TAKING NOTE
On a dig, palaeontologists always record details of a find, and draw a map of the site. Broken fragments and samples of rock are collected in bags and analysed later back in the laboratory.

HAMMERS
A variety of hammers are used by palaeontologists (fossil experts) in the field. The geological hammers shown here are good at splitting fossil-bearing rock.

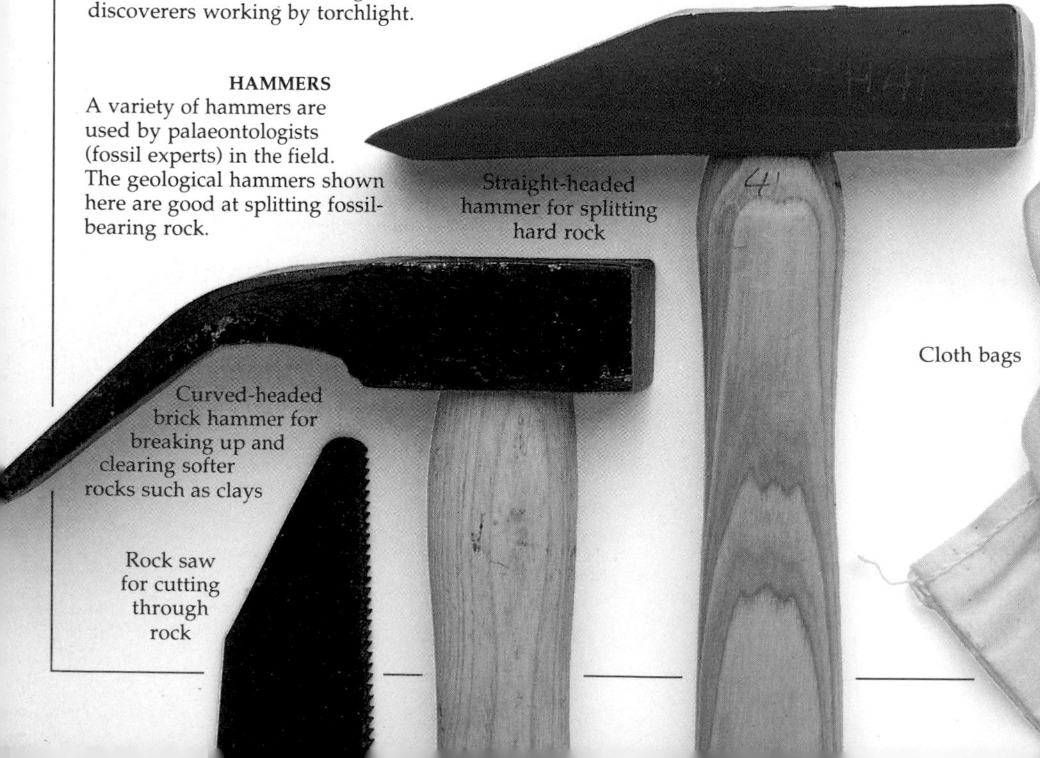

Straight-headed hammer for splitting hard rock

Curved-headed brick hammer for breaking up and clearing softer rocks such as clays

Rock saw for cutting through rock

Cloth bags

RIBS IN A JACKET
When fossils are partly exposed, they are sometimes encased in plaster jackets to protect them for transportation back to the laboratory. Two ribs of the recently discovered dinosaur *Baryonyx* can be seen in this jacket (pp. 54-55).

Hard hat and protective goggles

Pot of glue

POT AND BRUSHES
Brushes are used to clear away dust while rock is being chipped away around fossils. As a fossil is exposed, it is often painted with hardener, like glue, to secure any loose fragments.

Soft paintbrush

Lump hammer

Pointed chisels

Flat chisels

Plastic bags

EXPOSING A FIND
When the rock in which the fossil is embedded is very hard, a heavy hammer and chisels are needed. This lump hammer is used to drive chisels into the rock. It is useful to have a wide variety of chisels for getting into awkward corners.

Baryonyx ribs encased in plaster jacket

Aluminium foil covers fossil

PROTECTING THE FIND
A palaeontologist on a dig carefully covers a fossil with a plaster jacket.

FOAM JACKET
Sometimes fossils are protected by a polyurethane foam jacket. The fossil is first wrapped in foil, then the chemicals to make the foam are poured over it. The foam expands and surrounds the fossil, which can then be moved safely.
CAUTION: Foam gives off toxic gases as it is mixed, and is not recommended for use except by professionals.

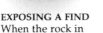

Clipboard with drawing of the site, and notebook with field notes

Hard paintbrush

Polyurethane foam jacket

RAW MATERIALS
To make a plaster jacket, the plaster is mixed with water to make a paste, then the scrim is dipped into it. A layer of wet tissue paper is used to cover the rock and fossil before plaster and scrim is applied. This prevents the plaster sticking to the rock and fossil.

Roll of plasterer's scrim (open-weave fabric), and plaster of Paris

How to rebuild a dinosaur

ᴀFTER THE HARD work of excavation, the precious fossils are taken back to the laboratory for preparation, study, and display. This whole process is a lengthy one. First, the fossil remains need to be carefully removed from their protective jackets (p. 53). Then, the remaining rock or earth in which the fossil was originally buried has to be cleaned away. Chisels are used on hard pieces of rock, or more delicate power-driven tools (like dentists' drills), for detailed work. Sometimes chemicals are used to dissolve away the surplus rock. The cleaned bones are then carefully studied in order to understand how they fitted together, and therefore how the dinosaur lived. Some tell-tale clues are to be found on the actual surface of bones, because muscles sometimes leave clear marks where they were attached. These marks can be used to reconstruct dinosaur muscles, or flesh.

ON DISPLAY
Museums often display fossil replicas, cast from moulds of the real, delicate fossils. This *Barosaurus* reproduction is being erected in the American Museum of Natural History. Not all scientists agree that *Barosaurus* could rear like this.

Iguanodon foot bone
Cartilage cap of ankle joint
Ligament scars

CLUES FROM THE BONE
This foot bone from *Iguanodon* provides many clues of muscle attachment during life. At the upper left end its surface is roughened for attachment of cartilage (gristle) of the ankle joint, and along its length are ligament scars for attachment to other bones. The rough area at the bottom of the bone is a cartilage joint surface for the middle toe.

Cartilage surface of joint for toe

Making a model

Many museums display cutaway reconstructions of dinosaurs, like the one below. The starting point is a scale drawing that details how the bones and muscles fitted together. Based on this, an armature (framework) is built from wire and wood. A sculptor shapes modelling clay around the armature, adding in details such as bones and skin texture. The clay model is used to create a rubber mould, so that a resin version can be cast. Finally, the cast is handpainted and airbrushed.

Preliminary sketch

Wire and wood armature

Finished clay model

Rubber mould

Painted and finished cast

DIGITAL DINOSAURS
Computers now create superb 3-D reconstructions of dinosaurs and other prehistoric creatures, such as this pareiasaur (right). Digital models can be viewed from all angles and even shown in motion.

Baryonyx neck
vertebra

Faint
scratches

A NECK BONE
This neck bone
belonged to the
newly discovered dinosaur
Baryonyx, seen reconstructed
below. The bone has a
very complicated shape and
was buried in very hard rock,
so it took a very long time to
prepare. The faint scratches
that can be seen are where
rock remains to be cleared.

A LOAD OF OLD BONES
During the 19th century, when dinosaurs had just been
discovered, (pp. 8-9), the sculptor Benjamin Waterhouse
Hawkins built models of dinosaurs first in Britain,
then in the United States. This shows his work-
shop in New York.

AN ACID BATH
Sometimes, in laboratories,
vats of acid are used to dissolve away rock from fossils
without damaging them. The
chemicals used in this process
can be very dangerous, so protective clothing must always be worn
when lowering the fossil into the vat.

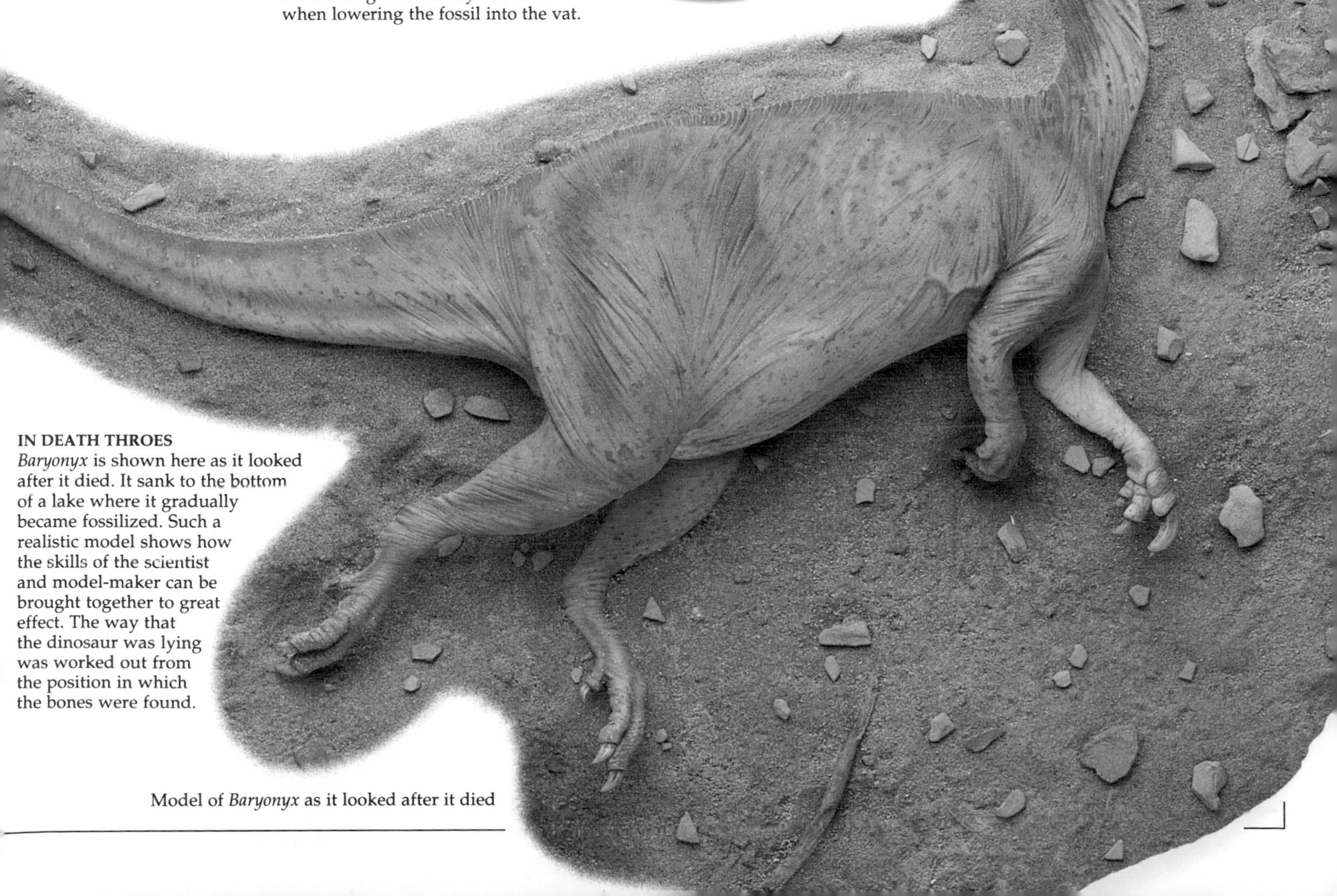

IN DEATH THROES
Baryonyx is shown here as it looked
after it died. It sank to the bottom
of a lake where it gradually
became fossilized. Such a
realistic model shows how
the skills of the scientist
and model-maker can be
brought together to great
effect. The way that
the dinosaur was lying
was worked out from
the position in which
the bones were found.

Model of *Baryonyx* as it looked after it died

The timescale

TRILOBITE
This creature lived on the sea bed and scuttled around on sharp, spiny legs. Although abundant in the early oceans, it was extinct long before the first dinosaurs appeared.

IT IS INCREDIBLE TO THINK that animals and plants have lived on this Earth for over 700 million years. During this time a bewildering variety has come and gone. The first dinosaurs appeared about 228 million years ago (mya) at the end of what is known as the Triassic Period. They roamed the Earth throughout the Jurassic Period until 65 million years ago, right at the end of the Cretaceous Period. During the millions of years of life on Earth, the world has changed enormously: continents have moved, sea levels have altered, climates have changed, creatures have become extinct. If we look at fossils of creatures that lived before, during, and after the dinosaur age, we can see how some things have changed, and some have remained much the same. At the time when the dinosaurs appeared, none of the countries of the world existed as we know them - the world consisted of one huge landmass called Pangaea.

IN THE MISTS OF TIME
This is what the word may have looked like during the dinosaur age. Dinosaurs lived through three periods of time: the Triassic, from 230 to 195 mya, the Jurassic, from 195 to 141 mya, and the Cretaceous, from 141 to 65 mya.

■ **260 mya:
AMPHIBIAN**
Amphibians lived before and during the dinosaur age, and are still with us today. Frogs, for instance, are amphibians. They can breathe and move on land, but have to lay their eggs in water (p. 44).

A BEETLE
Beetles are a group with a very long history, and were probably the prey of early reptiles and amphibians, just as they are today.

Small spiky teeth

■ **260 mya:
EARLY REPTILE**
This is the underside of the skull of an early lizard-like reptile, called *Captorhinus*. It may have eaten small insects and snails with its small spiky teeth.

■ **240 mya:
COELACANTH FISH**
The earliest known coelacanth appeared 390 million years ago. They were thought to be extinct, but recently many living coelacanths have been discovered.

Spaces for jaw muscles

■ **240 mya:
PROCOLOPHON**
This is the skull of a small early reptile which fed on roots and tubers.

SCORPION STORY
Living scorpions belong to an ancient group which dates back about 400 million years.

■ **240 mya:
DIICTODON**
Squat and pig-shaped, the owner of this mammal-like reptile skull ate plants and lived during the early Triassic Period.

LIVING FOSSIL
This lungfish has fossil relatives which date back 390 million years.

KEY: Green = pre- and post-dinosaur age; Red = dinosaur age.

■ 190 mya: MEGAZOSTRODON

This furry model is based on a tiny skeleton that was found a few years ago. It was one of the earliest true mammals, and lived alongside the early dinosaurs.

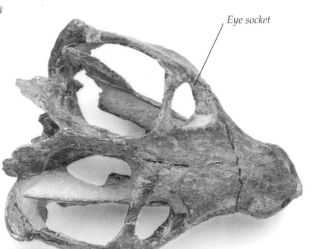

Eye socket

■ 235 mya: MASSETOGNATHUS

The last mammal-like reptiles that appeared just before the early dinosaurs were large and quite dog-like in appearance. Mammal-like reptiles became extinct when the dinosaurs appeared, but smaller, rodent-like mammals survived.

■ 225 mya: ■RIOJASUCHUS

This skull belonged to an immediate predecessor of the early dinosaurs, one of the thecodontian or "socket toothed" reptiles. It was built like a long-legged crocodile, and had powerful teeth and jaws.

■ 190 mya: ICHTHYOSAUR

Ichthyosaurs were swimming reptiles which flourished throughout the dinosaur age. This paddle - once a limb - would have been used by the animal to propel itself along in the water. Ichthyosaurs had long, narrow, pointed snouts.

Long narrow snout

■190 mya: CROCODILE

The shape of a crocodile skull has not changed very much over the years. Having a long snout lined with teeth is one of the best ways of catching swimming prey. The snout on this crocodile is particularly narrow, which suggests that it must have been very partial to fish.

The story continues...

Two *Thecodontosaurus* feeding

■ 210 mya: THECODONTOSAURUS

This fragment of jaw belonged to an early dinosaur. Most early dinosaur fossils are poorly preserved.

STAYING POWER
Crocodiles lived before, during and after the reign of the dinosaurs, and are still around today. Being aggressive river-dwelling predators obviously suits them very well.

EARLY DAYS
Thecodontosaurus could eat both plants and meat (p. 23). One of these two is feeding on cycads, while the other is about to pounce on a lizard.

■ **160 mya:**
CROCODILE
Crocodile scutes, or plates, like this square bony one are often found in rocks that also yield dinosaur remains. This suggests that crocodiles may have scavenged dinosaur carcasses.

■ **155 mya:**
PLESIOSAUR
This tooth belonged to a plesiosaur, a fierce predatory marine reptile, contemporary with ichthyosaurs (p. 57). They flourished in the sea during the Jurassic Period.

■**147 mya:** SPHENODONTID LIZARD
Lizard-like reptiles such as this specimen have a very long history. They lived throughout the reign of the dinosaurs.

Modern dragonfly

Fossil dragonfly

■ **140 mya:**
DATED DRAGONFLY
Dragonflies can be called "living fossils": they were flying in the skies 320 million years ago, and still exist today.

■**140 mya:**
KING CRAB
King crabs are only remotely related to crabs. They have been around since before the dinosaur age, and still live today.

■ **140 mya:**
GRYODUS
Many types of bony fish like this one lived at the same time as the dinosaurs. Most were fossilized in fine lake sediments, so are preserved in great detail.

■ **145 mya:**
PTERODACTYLUS
Flying reptiles called pterosaurs flew in the skies while the dinosaurs ruled the land. Some were the size of sparrows; others were as big as small aircraft. The larger ones would have swooped down to catch fish in the waters, while smaller ones, like this *Pterodactylus* (right), would have caught insects in the air.

Grey plover

DAWN OF THE BIRDS
The first birds appeared in the late Jurassic Period - about 150 mya. But they did not come into their own and dominate the skies until the pterosaurs became extinct (at the same time as the dinosaurs).

THE GREAT SURVIVOR

The cockroach is one of Nature's great survivors. Cockroaches have lived on Earth since long before the dinosaur age, and, judging by their success at living in human environments, they seem set to survive well into the future.

Cockroach

COME FLY. . .

In the Jurassic Period, a sky scene at dawn or dusk would have been crowded with pterosaurs darting through the air catching prey. Their place is taken today by birds that feed on the wing: swifts, housemartins, and swallows.

Water moccasin snake

SNAKES ON THE SCENE

Slithering snakes arrived on the scene in the late Cretaceous Period. They are like modified legless lizards.

■ 136 mya:
DRYOSAURUS
This femur (thigh bone) belonged to a small, fast-moving, plant-eating dinosaur. It used its speed to flee fierce predators.

Dryosaurus femur

■ 120 mya:
LIZARD'S JAW
This fragment of jaw came from a lizard like the sphenodontid preserved in rock, above left. Fragments like this are found more often than complete specimens.

■ 120 mya:
CROCODILE
The crocodile that owned this skull (right) lived in the early Cretaceous Period.

■ 115 mya:
IGUANODON
This is a tail bone from *Iguanodon*, a plant-eating dinosaur (pp. 8-9). *Iguanodon* lived only in the Cretaceous Period.

■ 120 mya: TEETH
These fierce-looking stumpy crocodile teeth are preserved from 120 million years ago, but are very like the teeth that belong to living crocodiles today.

The story continues. . .

■ 120 mya:
SCUTE
Part of a crocodile's bony armour, this scute comes from a crocodile that lived during the Cretaceous Period.

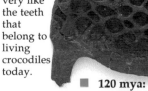

■ 110 mya:
GASTROPOD
Many different snails lived during the dinosaur age.

The end of an era

As the Cretaceous Period drew to a close, the dinosaurs became gradually less numerous, until eventually they disappeared altogether. At the same time changes were also taking place in the Earth's landscape. The continents became separated by wide stretches of sea. Sea levels rose also, flooding much of the low-lying land where many types of dinosaur lived. Many groups of sea animals became extinct. Instead of being warm all the time, the climate began to become more variable, or seasonal. The types of plants living at the time also changed: flowering plants became increasingly important. As the dinosaurs died out, they made way for a new ruling group on the Earth: the mammals.

Turtle shell

NOT LONG TO LIVE
The formidable mosasaurs only lived at the end of the Cretaceous Period, and became extinct alongside the dinosaurs.

■**70 mya:**
MOSASAUR
This giant marine lizard used its large pointed teeth to crack open shells of animals such as ammonites (p. 48).

■**90 mya:**
ALBERTOSAURUS
The owner of this toe bone was a large meat-eating dinosaur. Few of these meat eaters survived up to the end of the dinosaur age.

■**95 mya:**
TURTLE
This turtle shell is a relic from the Cretaceous Period. Turtles were another group that flourished instead of becoming extinct.

■**100 mya:**
ICHTHYOSAUR
Embedded in rock, these sharp, pointed teeth belonged to an ichthyosaur (p. 57). Marine reptiles like this all became extinct at the same time as the dinosaurs.

Scales

■**75 mya:**
CRAB
Closely related to the lobsters, crabs did not suffer extinction (p. 58).

Crab

■**85 mya:**
MARSUPIAL
This jaw bone belonged to a pouched mammal (like a kangaroo). Now found only in Australia, marsupials lived alongside the dinosaurs, and were able to evolve rapidly after they disappeared.

■**90 mya:**
BONY FISH
Bony ray-finned fish were another group that suffered very little damage during the "great extinction".

■**100 mya:**
LOBSTER
Some marine groups, like the lobsters, were little affected by the mass extinction that happened at the end of the Cretaceous Period. Why some groups were affected, and others not, is to this day a great mystery.

■**100 mya:**
LEAF
Broad leaves like this one are typical of flowering plants that appeared during the Cretaceous Period.

RED HERRING?
The bony fish we are familiar with today are very like those that lived in the late Cretaceous.

Hawksbill turtle

TURTLE TALE
Turtles and
tortoises belong to
a group of reptiles
that have changed
very little in appearance
since their origins 200
million years ago.

1 mya:
HOMO ERECTUS
Human beings were one of the last
species to arrive on the ever-
changing scene on Earth. Early
species of humans date back
a mere one million years
(64 million years after
the last dinosaur died).
In this "short" period
of time, people have
risen to dominate
most of the land,
and are
beginning to
have a notice-
able effect
on the
environment.

Human skull

25 mya:
SHARK TOOTH
Sharks have been
around for 400
million years,
and have
changed
very little.

55 mya:
TURTLE SKULL

Cricket

Spider

Hyracotherium
(early horse) skull

35 mya:
INSECTS IN AMBER
This cricket and
spider have been
perfectly preserved
from millions of years ago,
because they became trapped
in amber (fossilized resin)
exuding from
pine trees.

Early rodent skull

A BRACHIOPOD
One of the longest survivors of all
groups in nature, brachiopods,
or "lampshells", found today
are little changed from types
found in rocks 500
million years old.

35 mya:
EARLY RODENT
Gnawing animals like rats and
mice did not exist until well
after the dinosaurs died, and
are thriving today.

40 mya:
LIZARD
This jaw belonged to a land
lizard. Although all the
giant marine lizards like
mosasaurs (p. 59) became
extinct with the
dinosaurs, the small
land-living ones
were unaffected.

50 mya:
EARLY HORSE
Horses appeared soon after the
dinosaurs became extinct, and soon
there were many different types of
horse grazing upon the new plants
and grasses that were growing.
Early horses had toes, not hooves,
on their feet.

Red rose

FLOWER POWER
The flowering plants that appeared
early in the Cretaceous Period soon
begin to dominate the plant world.

THE BUZZING BEGINS
Brightly coloured flowers and flower scents seemed to
herald the arrival of butterflies and bees. Attracted by
the colours and scents of the flowers, butterflies, bees,
and other insects carried pollen from one to the other, just
like they do today.

Myths and legends

WHEN DINOSAUR BONES were first discovered, people found it hard to believe that these creatures had actually lived on Earth. The giant dinosaurs became linked with terrifying monsters in peoples' minds. Because so little was known about them, many mistakes were made at the beginning. Dinosaur bones were put together in the wrong way (p. 8), or even mixed up with other bones. Today, misconceptions about dinosaurs are just as common. Visitors to museums often think that the dinosaurs walked around looking like living skeletons! Politicians and commentators sometimes unfairly use dinosaurs to describe something that is old-fashioned, out of date, useless, or inefficient. It is common to think that dinosaurs were animals that were big, dull, stupid, and headed for extinction because they were poorly designed to cope with the world in which they lived. In fact, nothing could be further from the truth. Dinosaurs were among the most elegant and sophisticated animals that the Earth has ever seen, and survived for over 150 million years - 75 times longer than humans have lived on Earth.

DINOSAUR DRAGON
The winged dragon of mythology looks very like some dinosaurs, except for the wings. Some people see dragons and dinosaurs as being one and the same. But the big difference is that dragons never existed!

A WATERY END
A common mistake is to believe that dinosaurs were sea monsters, possibly still lurking in the ocean depths. In fact, no dinosaur was purely sea living. The sea reptiles that shared the dinosaur world were mostly plesiosaurs and ichthyosaurs.

DINOSAURS IN THE TREES
When *Hypsilophodon*, a small, agile, plant-eating dinosaur, was first discovered, it was thought to live in trees. Indeed, it was believed to be the dinosaur equivalent of a tree kangaroo that lives in Papua New Guinea. Scientists thought its long tail helped it to balance in the trees, while special sharp toes on its feet helped it to cling to branches. Now this theory has been proved wrong. In fact, *Hypsilophodon* was a ground-dwelling dinosaur that used its stiff tail as a stabilizer while running.

BRONTOSAURUS BLUNDERS
Scientists do the best they can with the evidence available, but early models of *Apatosaurus*, originally called *Brontosaurus*, were based on a mix-up. Its skeleton had been dug up but it lacked a skull, and its bones became muddled up with another sauropod, *Camarasaurus*. Museum reconstructions showed "*Brontosaurus*" with a short, round skull until the 1980s, when its real skull was found, proving to be very like the skull of *Diplodocus* (p. 22).

CHINESE DRAGONS
The mythical dragon is an important symbol in Chinese culture, and it seems likely that it originated from the discovery of dinosaur remains. The Chinese have been collecting dinosaur fossils for over 2,000 years, but referring to them as dragon bones. Even today "dragons' teeth" which are mostly fossil dinosaur teeth are collected and ground into powders for use as medicines, for they are thought to have healing properties.

Two *Hypsilophodon* dinosaurs perched in a tree

Special grasping toes

Balancing tail

Grasping hand to hold branch

DINOSAURS AND CAVE DWELLERS
Some films and cartoons have given the impression that dinosaurs shared the Earth with early people. In fact, dinosaurs became extinct 64 million years before the first people ever appeared on the Earth!

Did you know?

AMAZING FACTS

Iguanodon is one of the most common dinosaurs. In one location, between 1878–81, coal miners in Belgium dug up over 39 *Iguanodon* skeletons.

Baryonyx claw

One of the rarest dinosaurs known is *Baryonyx*. So far, only one specimen has been found. It includes a 30-cm (6-in)-long thumb claw.

Dinosaur fossils have been discovered in rocks from the Triassic Period. One of the earliest dinosaurs may have been *Eoraptor*, which was discovered in Argentina in 1991. Its name means "dawn (or early) plunderer lizard", because this meat-eater lived about 228 million years ago, at the beginning of the dinosaur era.

Remains of dinosaurs have been discovered in Madagascar, Africa, which may be older than *Eoraptor*, at around 234 million years old. However, the remains are in poor condition and scientists are still debating the find.

The earliest-known carnosaur is *Piatnitzkysaurus*, from the Jurassic Period.

Fossilized skin of *Saltasaurus*

The first dinosaur named was the carnosaur, *Megalosaurus*, in 1824.

The name ornithomimid means "bird-mimic reptile" because scientists think these dinosaurs were built like flightless, long-legged birds such as ostriches.

All that scientists knew of *Troodon* for several years was a single tooth – the name "troodontid" means "wounding tooth".

Troodon is the best-known troodontid. It had large eyes and a relatively large brain for its body size, giving it the reputation of being one of the most intelligent dinosaurs and a successful hunter. Scientists base this theory on the similarity of the optic nerve channels and brain cases of fossils with those of modern predatory creatures.

Troodontid fossils are rare, partly because their thin bones were not easily preserved.

Dromaeosaurid means "running lizard" and these small, aggressive hunters were probably both swift and lethal, with their blade-like fangs, clawed hands, and huge switchblade claws on their second toes.

Fossils of the small plant-eater *Protoceratops* are so abundant in the Gobi Desert in Mongolia, that fossil-hunting palaeontologists there call it the "sheep of the Gobi".

A tangled fossil found in the Gobi Desert in 1971 shows a *Protoceratops* and a *Velociraptor* fighting. The *Velociraptor* had grasped the plant-eater's snout while kicking its throat. The *Protoceratops* had gripped its attacker's arm in its strong beak. The animals may have died from their wounds or been killed by a fall of sand from a nearby dune.

Scientists used to think that the ankylosaurs were the only armoured dinosaurs until the discovery of an armoured sauropod, *Saltasaurus*. Its armour consisted of large bony plates covered by smaller, bony nodules, and probably covered its back and sides.

Coprolites – preserved dung – contain the remains of what dinoaurs ate, such as bone fragments, fish scales, or the remains of plants. Scientists can study them to find out about dinosaur diets.

A dinosaur egg can only be firmly identified if an embryo is preserved in it. So far, this has only been possible with *Troodon, Hypacrosaurus, Maiasaura, Oviraptor* and, recently, a titanosaur (see next page).

The first complete titanosaur skeleton was found in Madagascar in July 2001. Titanosaurs grew to around 15 m (50 ft) long but their bones were relatively light, so few have survived.

Tyrannosaurus had the reputation of being the largest meat-eater for many years, but lost out in 1993 when an even larger meat-eater (*Giganotosaurus carolinii*) was discovered in southern Argentina.

Giganotosaurus is thought to have been as heavy as 125 people, with a head twice the size of that of *Allosaurus*.

Large eyes absorb more light, improving night vision

Troodon

Dinosaur footprints are far more common than fossil dinosaur bones. They are often given their own scientific names because it is difficult to tell which particular animal made a particular footprint.

Few dinosaur tracks show the marks of a tail, which suggests that dinosaurs walked with their tails held off the ground.

QUESTIONS AND ANSWERS

Q How many types of dinosaur are there?

A So far, about 700 species of dinosaur have been named. However, half of these are based on incomplete skeletons, so some may not be separate species. About 540 dinosaur genera have been named. Of this number, about 300 are considered to be valid genera. Most genera contain only one species, but some have more. Some scientists believe that there may be 800 or so dinosaur genera still to be discovered.

Q How are dinosaurs named?

A Dinosaurs may be named after a feature of ther bodies (such as *Triceratops*, meaning three-horned face), the place where they were found (such as *Argentinosaurus*), or after a person involved in the discovery, such as *Herrerasaurus*

Titanosaur eggs

(Herrera's lizard). An animal name usually consists of the genus and the species name. For example, the biological name for humans is *Homo* (genus) *sapiens* (species).

Q How did dinosaurs communicate?

A Scientists believe that dinosaurs probably communicated through sound and visual displays. The chambered crests on the heads of some dinosaurs, such as *Parasaurolophus*, may have amplified grunts or calls. It is thought that forest-living dinosaurs made high-pitched sounds that carried through the trees. Those that lived on the plains may have made low-pitched sounds that would carry well along the ground. Visual displays could have including posturing, such as pawing the ground or shaking the head.

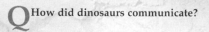
Psittacosaurus, meaning "parrot lizard"

Q Were dinosaurs warm- or cold-blooded?

A The debate still rages about whether dinosaurs were warm-blooded, like mammals, or cold-blooded, like reptiles. Swift and agile predators, such as *Deinonychus*, would indicate a warm-blooded mode of life. Also, some dinosaurs have now been found with feathers, and only warm-blooded animals would need such insulation. However, some dinosaurs, such as *Stegosaurus*, had plates on their backs, possibly to collect heat from the Sun, which suggests they were cold-blooded. In 2000, research was published on the discovery of the first-ever fossilized dinosaur heart (in 1993). Many scientists dispute the findings. However, the research suggests that the heart was similar to those of birds and different from those of modern-day reptiles, so some dinosaurs at least were probably warm-blooded.

Q What colour were the dinosaurs?

A Palaeontologists do not know for sure, but they think that most dinosaurs may have been as brightly coloured as modern-day reptiles (such as snakes and lizards) and birds. Some may have had patterned skin to help them hide in vegetation. Others may have had bright warning colours to scare off predators or as a kind of display to help them find a mate.

Q Who found thousands of dinosaur eggs?

A In 1997, a group of Argentinian and American scientists discovered thousands of grapefruit-sized rocks littering a dry, barren area in Patagonia, South America. As they neared the site, they realized the "rocks" were fossilized dinosaur eggs. Some of the eggs contained embryos, so the scientists were able to work out that the unborn babies were probably titanosaurs. The mothers would have returned to the same nesting grounds each year.

Record Breakers

BIGGEST DINOSAUR
Seismosaurus ("earth-shaking lizard") probably measured around 34 m (110 ft) and weighed up to 30 tonnes (29.5 tons). Some scientists believe *Argentinosaurus* was ever larger overall, weighing 50 tonnes (49 tons). However, skeletons of both are incomplete.

BIGGEST MEAT-EATER
Theropods *Giganotosaurus* ("huge lizard") and *Carcharodontosaurus* ("shark-toothed lizard") were both nearly 14 m (46 ft) long.

BIGGEST HEAD
Including its head shield, the head of ceratopian *Torosaurus* measured 2.8 m (9 ft) long – longer than a saloon car.

LONGEST NECK
The neck of *Mamenchisaurus* measured up to 9.8 m (32 ft) and contained 19 vertebrae, making up almost half of the animal's total body length.

SMALLEST BRAIN
Stegosaurus had the smallest brain of any known dinosaur. It weighed about 70 g (2.5 oz) and was the size of a walnut.

LONGEST DINOSAUR NAME
Micropachycephalosaurus

SHORTEST DINOSAUR NAME
Minmi

Stegosaurus

Classification of dinosaurs

ALL LIVING THINGS ARE CLASSIFIED into different groups, according to their common features. The classification of dinosaurs, however, is controversial and continually revised as new discoveries are made and existing evidence is reinterpreted. In this chart, dinosaurs are subdivided into two main groups – Saurischia (lizard-hipped dinosaurs) and Ornithischia (bird-hipped dinosaurs). Each group is then subdivided into the levels of families (with names ending in "-idae"), genera (indicated in the chart below in italics), and species. Birds (Aves) are now generally considered to be the descendants of the dinosaurs.

ORNITHISCHIA

Hypsilophodon,
an ornithischian

CERAPODA

THYREOPHORA

Pisanosaurus

Lesothosaurus

Lesothosaurus, a
primitive ornithischian

Stegoceras, a
pachycephalosaur

Iguanodon,
an ornithopod

MARGINOCEPHALIA

STEGOSAURIA

ANKYLOSAURIA

ORNITHOPODA	CERATOPIA	PACHYCEPHALOSAURIA	*Scelidosaurus* *Scutellosaurus*	Huayangosauridae Stegosauridae	Ankylosauridae Nodosauridae
Camptosauridae Dryosauridae Hadrosauridae Heterodontosauridae Hypsilophodontidae Iguanodontidae	Ceratopidae Protoceratopidae Psittacosauridae	Chaoyoungosauridae Homalocephalidae Pachycephalosauridae			

Scelidosaurus,
a thyreophoran

Triceratops,
a ceratopian

Edmontonia,
a nodosaurid

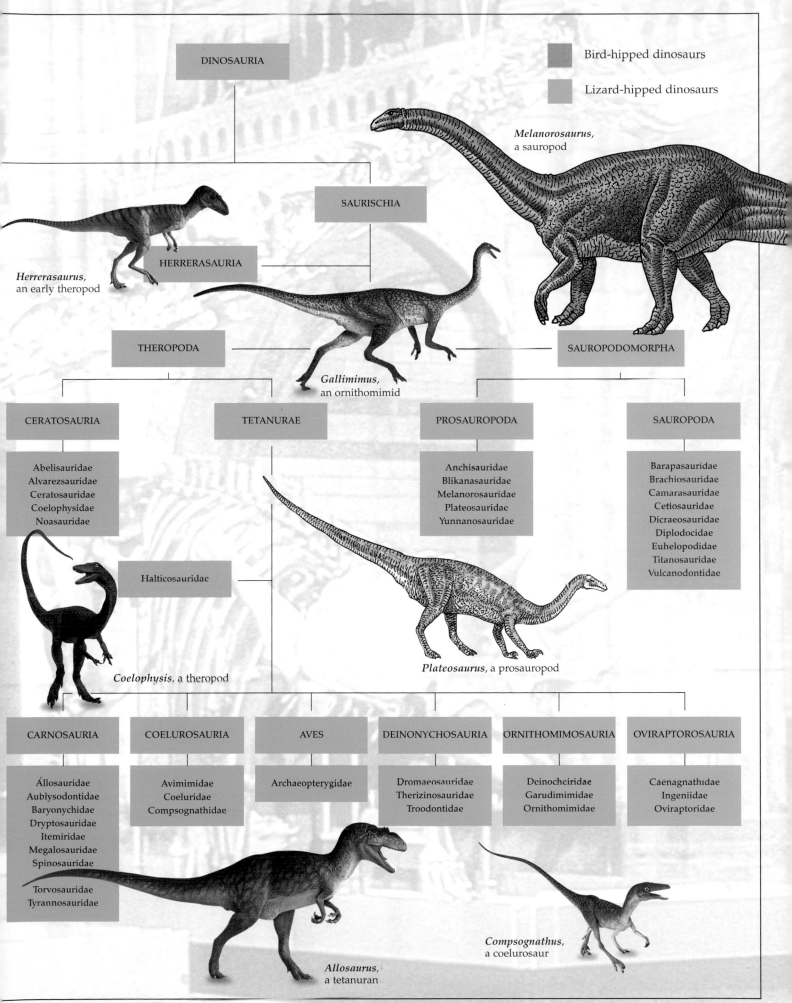

DINOSAURIA

Bird-hipped dinosaurs

Lizard-hipped dinosaurs

Melanorosaurus, a sauropod

SAURISCHIA

HERRERASAURIA

Herrerasaurus, an early theropod

THEROPODA

SAUROPODOMORPHA

Gallimimus, an ornithomimid

CERATOSAURIA

TETANURAE

PROSAUROPODA

SAUROPODA

Abelisauridae
Alvarezsauridae
Ceratosauridae
Coelophysidae
Noasauridae

Anchisauridae
Blikanasauridae
Melanorosauridae
Plateosauridae
Yunnanosauridae

Barapasauridae
Brachiosauridae
Camarasauridae
Cetiosauridae
Dicraeosauridae
Diplodocidae
Euhelopodidae
Titanosauridae
Vulcanodontidae

Halticosauridae

Coelophysis, a theropod

Plateosaurus, a prosauropod

CARNOSAURIA	COELUROSAURIA	AVES	DEINONYCHOSAURIA	ORNITHOMIMOSAURIA	OVIRAPTOROSAURIA
Allosauridae Aublysodontidae Baryonychidae Dryptosauridae Itemiridae Megalosauridae Spinosauridae Torvosauridae Tyrannosauridae	Avimimidae Coeluridae Compsognathidae	Archaeopterygidae	Dromaeosauridae Therizinosauridae Troodontidae	Deinocheiridae Garudimimidae Ornithomimidae	Caenagnathidae Ingeniidae Oviraptoridae

Compsognathus, a coelurosaur

Allosaurus, a tetanuran

Find out more

MANY PEOPLE ARE SO FASCINATED by dinosaurs that even though these amazing creatures died out millions of years ago and no human has even seen one, there are plenty of places to find out more about them. Museums of natural history or specialist dinosaur museums display life-sized reconstructions, often with sound effects or moving parts. You can also take a virtual tour of many museums over the internet if you cannot visit them in person. Television programmes, such as the BBC's *Walking with Dinosaurs*, or films such as *Jurassic Park* also give fascinating and realistic portrayals of the age of the dinosaurs.

GO FOSSIL HUNTING
A great deal of research is made before any organized fossil-hunting expeditions by palaeontologists. Even so, some important dinosaur discoveries have been made by amateur fossil-hunters where fossil-bearing rocks have been exposed. Eroding cliffs are the best places to find fossils, especially on seashores. Before starting any such search, collectors must make sure they get permission to visit a site if necessary. Care must also be taken at coastal sites to stay away from overhangs and watch for the incoming tide.

Realistic dinosaur model from the BBC film The Lost World, *based on the novel by Sir Arthur Conan Doyle, filmed in New Zealand in 2001*

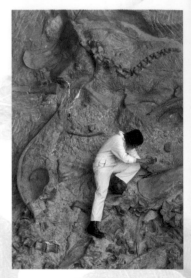

ON A DINO DIG
It is possible to arrange to go on an actual dinosaur dig or watch scientists at work in the field. For example, at the Dinosaur National Monument Quarry in Utah, the United States (right), visitors can see excavation of fossils in progress. The Wyoming Dinosaur Centre also offers dig tours where you can join palaeotechnicians on an active dinosaur dig. For more information, log on to their website at http://server1.wyodino.org/index.

SEE A FILM!
Recent films and television programmes use computer-generated imagery (in which many of the visuals are created and animated by computer software) to portray dinosaurs. *Jurassic Park* was the first film to employ palaeontologists as advisers and to present dinosaurs as realistically as possible. Before then, dinosaurs were brought to life for the screen by such methods as sticking horns on lizards (*Journey to the Centre of the Earth*, 1958), or manipulating puppets off-screen (*The Land That Time Forgot*, 1974).

Computer animatronics bring a herd of stampeding dinosaurs to life in the third *Jurassic Park* film.

Full-sized mechanical model of an allosaur, used for close-up shots in The Lost World *in conjunction with computer-generated images*

BEHIND THE SCENES
Original fossil bones are extremely heavy so modern reconstructions usually use lightweight casts to make the mounting easier. The original bones are then housed in museum storerooms and used for research purposes. Many museums have laboratories, where scientists study dinosaurs and other fossils. Some museums offer visitors the opportunity of watching scientists at work.

Diplodocus skeleton, on display in the entrance hall of the Natural History Museum, London

New thinking suggests that Diplodocus would not have been able to raise its long neck higher than its shoulders

VISIT A MUSEUM
Dinosaurs are often the most popular exhibits in natural history museums. Collections usually include full-size reconstructions to give people an impression of how dinosaurs might have looked when they were alive. Some museums have computer-animated models that move realistically, with sound effects. Look out, too, for travelling exhibitions from other museums, giving you the opportunity of seeing dinosaurs discovered in different parts of the world.

USEFUL WEBSITES

- Plenty of facts for serious dinosaur enthusiasts:
  www.dinodata.org/
- Website of the natural History Museum in London:
  www.nhm.ac.uk
- BBC educational site with plenty of dinosaur data:
  www.bbc.co.uk/sn/prehistoric_life/index.shtml
- For a virtual tour of the famous fossil halls at the American Museum of Natural History:
  www.amnh.org
- The Field Museum of Natural History's Dino Zone:
  www.fmnh.org
- Tour the Smithsonian Museum's dinosaur galleries:
  www.nmnh.si.edu/paleo/dino/

Sue's mouth was filled with long, pointed teeth; she may also have suffered from toothache – five holes in her lower jaw are thought to be places of infection

SEE "SUE"
"Sue" is the name given to the largest and most complete skeleton of a tyrannosaur ever discovered. It was found by Sue Hendrickson in 1990, and bought by the Chicago Field Museum. "Sue" went on display in 2000. Except for the skull, the skeleton on display is the real thing (not a plaster cast or plastic model). The bones were so well-preserved, you can see fine details where soft tissue, such as muscles or tendons, were attached.

Places to visit

NATURAL HISTORY MUSEUM
Cromwell Road, London
Touch-screens, interactive exhibits, and videos help you learn about prehistoric life. Highlights include:
- robotic dinosaurs, especially the realistic animatronic *Tyrannosaurus rex*
- a model *Maiasaura* nest complete with hatchlings
- a huge 26-m (85-ft) long skeleton of *Diplodocus*

DINOSAUR ISLE
Yaverland, Isle of Wight
First purpose-built dinosaur museum in Europe where several important finds have been made. It includes:
- an animatronic *Neovenator* – a meat-eater than once roamed the Isle of Wight
- the opportunity of going on fossil walks and watching scientists at work

AMERICAN MUSEUM OF NATURAL HISTORY
Central Park West, New York
Famous for its series of fossil halls, this museum currently has the largest number of dinosaur skeletons on display. Highlights include:
- *Tyrannosaurus, Apatosaurus,* and *Maniraptor* skeletons
- the only cast of a juvenile *Stegoceras* ever to have been found
- skin impressions of *Edmontosaurus* and *Corythosaurus*

FIELD MUSEUM OF NATURAL HISTORY
Lake Shore Drive, Chicago
The museum has exhibits covering 3.8 billion years of life on Earth and includes:
- specimens from every major dinosaur group, including a *Cryolophosaurus,* one of the first dinosaurs found in Antarctica
- "Sue", the world's largest and best-preserved *Tyrannosaurus*
- remains of some early dinosaurs discovered in Madagascar, which may be older than *Herrerasaurus* and *Eoraptor*

SMITHSONIAN MUSEUM OF NATURAL HISTORY
Washington, DC
This is one of the largest collections in the United States and highlights include:
- dioramas recreating scenes from the Jurassic and Cretaceous periods
- a discovery room where you are allowed to handle fossils
- a Fossil Laboratory, where you can arrange to watch scientists at work

DINOSAUR NATIONAL MONUMENT QUARRY
Utah, USA
Sited where some of the largest finds from the Jurassic Period have been discovered, highlights include:
- the opportunity of watching scientists at work in the field
- displays of some of the North American dinosaurs made here, including long-neck, plant-eating sauropods
- a sandstone cliff in which over 1,600 bones have been exposed, which makes up one wall of the Visitor's Centre

Glossary

ALLOSAUR ("strange lizard") Primitive tetanuran theropod (large meat-eating dinosaur).

AMMONITE One of an extinct group of cephalopods with a coiled, chambered shell that lived in Mesozoic seas.

AMPHIBIAN Cold-blooded vertebrate originating in the Carboniferous Period, whose young use gills to breathe during the early stages of life. Living amphibians include frogs, newts, and salamanders.

ANKYLOSAUR ("fused lizard") Four-legged, armoured, plant-eating, ornithischian dinosaur with bony plates covering the neck, shoulders and back, and a horny beak used for cropping plants.

AVES Birds, which probably evolved from theropod dinosaurs in the Late Jurassic Period. Some scientists only use "Aves" for modern birds, calling the most primitive birds "Avialae".

BIPEDAL Walking on two hindlimbs, rather than on all fours.

BRACHIOPOD Marine invertebrate with a two-valved shell, which evolved in the Cambrian Period.

CARNIVORE Meat-eating mammal with sharp teeth, such as a cat, dog, bear, or one of their relatives and ancestors; sometimes used to describe all meat-eating animals.

CARNOSAUR Large meat-eating dinosaur with a big skull and teeth. The name was once used for all such theropods but is now restricted to *Allosaurus* and its relatives.

Hadrosaur (*Corythosaurus*)

CEPHALOPOD Marine mollusc with large eyes and well-developed head ringed by tentacles, such as an octopus, squid or cuttlefish.

CERATOPIAN or CERATOPSIAN ("horned face") Bipedal and quadrupedal plant-eating ornithischian dinosaur, with a deep beak and a bony frill at the back of its skull.

CERATOSAUR ("horned lizard") One of two major groups of theropods.

COLD-BLOODED Depending upon the heat from the sun for body warmth. (*see also* WARM-BLOODED)

CONIFER Tree that bears cones, such as a pine or fir.

COPROLITE Fossilized dung.

Fossil of a plesiosaur flipper

CRETACEOUS PERIOD Third period of the Mesozoic Era, 145-65 million years ago.

CYCAD Palm-like, seed-bearing plant with long fern-like leaves.

DIPLODOCID ("double beam") Plant-eating sauropod; one of a family of huge saurischian dinosaurs with long necks and long tails.

DROMAEOSAURID ("running lizard") Bird-like, bipedal, carnivorous dinosaur.

DUCKBILLED DINOSAUR (*see* HADROSAUR)

EMBRYO Plant or an unborn animal in an early stage of development.

EVOLUTION The process by which one species gives rise to another. Evolution occurs when individual organisms pass on mutations (chance changes in genes controlling body size, shape, colour, and so on). Individuals with beneficial mutations pass them on. Their kind multiplies, and new species arise.

Ginko

EXTINCTION The dying-out of a plant or animal species.

FOSSIL The remains of something that once lived, preserved in rock. Teeth and bones are more likely to form fossils than softer body parts, such as internal organs.

GASTROLITH Stones swallowed by some animals, such as sauropods, to help grind up food in the stomach.

GENUS (plural, GENERA) Group of related organisms, ranked between the levels of family and species.

GINGKO Deciduous tree that grows to around 25 m (115 ft) in height, which evolved in the Triassic Period and survives essentially unchanged to this day.

HADROSAUR ("bulky lizard") Duck-billed dinosaur; large, bipedal/quadrupedal ornithopod from the Late Cretaceous Period with a duck-like beak used for browsing on vegetation.

HERBIVORE Animal that feeds on plants.

IGUANODONTIAN ("Iguana teeth") Large, bipedal/quadrupedal plant-eating ornithopod from the Early Cretaceous Period. (*see also* ORNITHOPOD)

INVERTEBRATE Animal without a backbone.

JURASSIC Second period of the Mesozoic Era, 200–145 million years ago.

MAMMAL Warm-blooded, hairy vertebrate that suckles its young.

MANIRAPTORAN ("grasping hands") Tetanuran theropod with long arms and hands, including predatory dinosaurs such as *Velociraptor*, and birds.

MEGALOSAUR ("great lizard") Primitive tetanuran theropod, less advanced than an allosaur.

MESOZOIC "Middle life" geological era about 250–65 million years ago, containing the Triassic, Jurassic and Cretaceous periods; and the "Age of the Dinosaurs". Dinosaurs became extinct at the end of the era.

ORNITHISCHIAN ("bird hips") One of two main dinosaur groups. In ornithischian dinosaurs, the pelvis is similar to that of birds. (see also SAURISCHIAN)

ORNITHOPOD ("bird feet") Bipedal ornithischian dinosaur with long hindlimbs.

OVIRAPTORID ("egg stealer") Maniraptoran theropod dinosaur with a beak and long legs.

PACHYCEPHALOSAUR ("thick-headed lizard") Bipedal ornithischian dinosaur with a thick skull.

Cycad

PALAEONTOLOGIST Someone who studies palaeontology.

PALAEONTOLOGY The scientific study of fossilized plants and animals.

PALAEOZOIC "Ancient life" geological era from 540–240 million years ago, containing the Cambrian, Ordovician, Silurian, Devonian, Carboniferous, and Permian periods.

PLESIOSAUR Large Mesozoic marine reptile with flipper-shaped limbs and (often) a long neck.

PREDATOR Animal or plant that preys on animals for food.

PRESERVATION Keeping something (such as a fossil) free from harm or decay.

PROSAUROPOD Early plant-eating saurischian dinosaur that lived from the Late Triassic to Early Jurassic eras.

PSITTACOSAUR ("parrot lizard") Ceratopian ornithischian plant-eater from the Cretaceous Period. A psittacosaur was bipedal with a deep, parrot-like beak.

PTEROSAUR ("winged lizard") Flying reptile of the Mesozoic Era, related to the dinosaurs.

QUADRUPEDAL Walking on all fours.

REPTILE Cold-blooded, scaly vertebrate that reproduces by laying eggs or giving birth on land. Living reptiles include lizards, snakes, turtles, and crocodiles.

SAURISCHIAN ("lizard hips") One of two main dinosaur groups. In saurischian dinosaurs, the pelvis is similar to that of lizards (see also ORNITHISCHIAN)

SAUROPOD ("lizard feet") Huge, plant-eating quadrupedal saurischian dinosaur that lived through most of the Mesozoic Era.

SAUROPODOMORPH ("lizard foot form") Large plant-eating quadrupedal saurischian dinosaur, including the prosauropods and sauropods.

SCUTE Bony plate with a horny covering set into an animal's skin to protect it from an enemy's teeth and claws.

SEDIMENT Material deposited by wind, water, or ice.

SKULL The head's bony framework protecting the brain, eyes, ears, and nasal passages.

SPECIES The level below genus in the classification of living things. Individuals in a species can breed to produce fertile young.

STEGOSAUR ("plated/roofed lizard") Plant-eating, quadrupedal ornithischian dinosaur with two tall rows of bony plates running down its neck, back, and tail.

TETANURAN ("stiff tail") One of the two main groups of theropod dinosaurs.

THECODONT ("socket teeth") One of a mixed group of archosaurs, which includes dinosaurs, crocodiles, and pterosaurs.

THEROPOD ("beast feet") One of a group of predatory dinosaurs with sharp teeth and claws.

TITANOSAUR ("gigantic lizard") Huge, quadrupedal plant-eating sauropod.

TRACE FOSSIL Trace left by a prehistoric creature, such as its footprints, eggs, bite marks, droppings, and fossil impressions of skin, hair, and feathers.

Dromaeosaurid (*Velociraptor*)

TRIASSIC First period of the Mesozoic Era, about 250–200 million years ago.

TYRANNOSAURID ("tyrant lizard") Huge, bipedal carnivorous tetanuran theropod characterized by a large head, short arms, two-fingered hands, and massive hindlimbs; flourished during the Late Cretaceous Period in North America and Asia.

WARM-BLOODED Keeping body temperature at a constant level, often above or below that of the surrounding environment, by turning energy from food into heat. (see also COLD-BLOODED)

Theropod
(*Therizinosaurus*)

Index

Acknowledgements

Dorling Kindersley would like to thank:
Angela Milner & the staff of the British Museum (Natural History); Kew Gardens & Clifton Nurseries for advice & plant specimens; Trevor Smith's Animal World; The Institute of Vertebrate Palaeoanthropology, Beijing, for permission to photograph Chinese dinosaurs; Brian Carter for obtaining plant specimens; Victoria Sorzano for typing; William Lindsay for advice on pp52-53 & pp 54-55; Fred Ford & Mike Pilley of Radius Graphics; Richard Czapnik for design; Dave King for special photography on pp6-7 & pp10-11; Jane Parker for the index.

For this edition, the publisher would also like to thank: Professor Michael Benton for assisting with revisions; Steve Setford for editorial assistance; Rose Horridge, Myriam Megharbi, & Sarah Smithies for picture research; Claire Bowers, David Ekholm–JAlbum, Sunita Gahir, Joanne Little, Nigel Ritchie, Susan St Louis, Carey Scott, & Bulent Yusef for the clipart; David Ball, Neville Graham, Rose Horridge, Joanne Little, & Sue Nicholson for the wallchart.

The publisher would like to thank the following for their kind permission to reproduce their images:

Picture credits t=top, b=bottom, m=middle, l=left, r=right

Alamy Images: Greg Vaughn 49b;
American Museum of Natural History: 44bl, 54tl; /C. Chesak 42bl;
ANT/NHPA: 7tr;
Artia Foreign Trade Corporation: /Zdenek Burian 10m;
BBC Hulton Picture Library: 8tl, 9tm, 31t;
The Bridgeman Art Library: 17bl;
The British Museum (Natural History): 52tl, 52ml, 55tr;
Bruce Coleman Ltd: 14-15; /Jane Burton 6ml, 13br, 29ml, 35tl, 36tl, 39tr, 50tl, 57bl, 59tl; /Janos Jurka 34tl;
Corbis: 69b; /James L. Amos 68mr; /Tom Bean 64-65; /Derek Hall/Frank Lane Picture Agency 68tl;
Jules Cowan: 51bl (background only);

Albert Dickson: 46bl;
DK Images: Graham High 70bl; Jon Hughes 42bl, 71br; Jon Hughes/Bedrock Studios 48bl; Natural History Museum, London 18–19 (tail), 19bl, 19tl, 19tr, 42, 42tl, 42–43tc, 43r, 48cl, 48cra, 48–49cb, 50br; Luis Rey 71cra; /Senckenberg, Forschungsinstitut und Naturmuseum, Frankfurt 50bl, 50crb; The South Florida Museum of Natural History 51tc, 51tr;
Alistair Duncan: 71ml;
Robert Harding: 63tr;
The Illustrated London News: 46tl;
The Image Bank: /L. Castaneda 15mr;
The Kobal Collection: 63m; Dreamworks/Paramount 49tl; Jurassic Park III © ILM (Industrial Light & Magic) 68bl;
The Mansell Collection: 28tl, 42mr, 56tr;
Mary Evans Picture Library: 9bl, 9m, 12tl, 16bl, 25ml, 34ml, 35bm, 62tl, 62bl, 62mr;
Museo Arentino De Cirendas Naterales, Buenos Aires: 64bl;
The Natural History Museum, London: 23bl, 64tl, 65tm, 68-69;
Natural Science Photos: /Arthur Hayward 24tr, 29bl, 37tr; /G. Kinns 30tl; /C.A. Walker 40tl;
David Norman: 53mr;
Planet Earth Pictures: /Richard Beales 32tl;

/Ken Lucas 31mr;
Rex Features: 66-67, 69m; /Simon Runtin 68br;
Royal Tyrrel Museum, Canada: 66mr, 70-71;
Science Photo Library: /David A. Hardy 49tl; /Philippe Plailly/Eurelios 65ml, 69t.

Picture research: Angela Murphy, Celia Dearing

Illustrations by:
Bedrock: 12m, 14tl;
Angelika Elsebach: 21tl, 36b;
Sandie Hill: 20br, 28tr, 44tr;
Mark Iley: 18bl;
Malcolm McGregor: 43bl;
Richard Ward: 26bm, 47b;
Ann Winterbotham: 10tl;
John Woodcock: 6tr, 7mr, 14b, 14ml;

Wallchart:
DK Images: Luis Rey br.

All other images © Dorling Kindersley
For further information see:
www.dkimages.com